Cyril Harris

Chrysanthemums

illustrated by James Nickalls

Hamlyn · London
Sun Books · Melbourne

FOREWORD

It has been said that the popularity of a plant is determined by its versatility. Certainly chrysanthemums must be high up in any chart that measures this quality. The majority of gardeners are interested in them because there are so many places in the garden that they can effectively fill, and there is a type or cultivar to meet every situation. For indoor decorations they are equally popular. Perhaps in this area, at least in terms of volume, chrysanthemums excel, particularly in more recent years since new techniques have made it possible to obtain them, both as cut flowers and pot plants, throughout the year. Lastly, apart from roses, there is no other plant that is seen so frequently on the show bench. Their popularity is reflected by the fact that the National Chrysanthemum Society runs two large-scale national shows annually.

Although this book has been written mainly for the beginner, it is hoped that the more experienced grower will find it both helpful and interesting.

My thanks go to the artist Mr. J. Nickalls for his excellent work in helping to create this book. I would also like to express my sincere gratitude to Mr. S. G. Gosling, Secretary of the National Chrysanthemum Society, and to Mr. L. Steadman, Chairman of the High Wycombe Chrysanthemum Society, for their valuable assistance. Finally, I would like to mention two nurseries, Sutton's of Reading and Carlisle's of Twyford, for affording facilities to the artist.

C.C.H.

Published by The Hamlyn Publishing Group Limited
London · New York · Sydney · Toronto
Hamlyn House, Feltham, Middlesex, England
In association with Sun Books Pty Ltd Melbourne

SBN 600 00085 0
Phototypeset by Jolly & Barber Limited, Rugby, England
Colour separations by Schwitter Limited, Zurich
Printed in England by Sir Joseph Causton & Sons Limited

CONTENTS

4 Introduction
8 The chrysanthemum family
22 Preparing to grow
chrysanthemums
22 Acquiring a collection
24 Foods and fertilizers
35 Potting composts
41 After-care of stools
43 Propagation
54 Stopping, timing,
securing and disbudding
59 Cultivating early-
flowering varieties
83 Weather protection
86 Chrysanthemums for
garden display
98 Late-flowering
chrysanthemums
122 Chrysanthemum diseases
130 Chrysanthemum pests
140 Exhibiting
chrysanthemums
150 Chrysanthemums
all the year round
152 Monthly programme
156 Books to read
157 Index

INTRODUCTION

Chrysanthemums owe a great deal of their popularity to their outstanding versatility of purpose, size and effect. There are the dwarfs, which often do not exceed 8 inches in height, packed with blooms of the loveliest hues, making ample provision for window boxes, pots and forward positions in garden borders. Formality and dignity are represented by those lovely exhibition varieties with enormous blooms, at least ten inches in diameter. Then there are the giants, like the species *Chrysanthemum uliginosum* with its white flowers, towering no less than seven feet in height to form an excellent background to a herbaceous border.

Much of the fascination of chrysanthemums lies in the wide range of type, size and shape found in their blooms, with a delightful range of colour. There are the splendid incurved, the spectacular reflexed decoratives, the formal colourful pin-cushion-like pompons, the flowering cascades, the spidery

A variety of dwarfed chrysanthemums.

rayonnantes, the intriguing azalea-like *Chrysanthemum azalea-num*, the all-purpose single flowered Koreans, and so many others. Every colour is represented, except true blue. Within the flowers themselves, the variety of petal shapes contributes substantially to the exquisite delight they give. The diameters of chrysanthemum blooms range from less than an inch to ten inches or more.

Perhaps it is the wide variance of their purpose which adds most to their popularity. Practically every need can be met by them. They give colour to a rockery in summer, provide a background to a herbaceous border and fill the shrubbery at a time when many other occupants are becoming rather jaded. For town house and flat-dwellers, there are cultivars, for which there is no equal to adorn window boxes and tubs. The most important purpose, however, is the provision of blooms for exhibitions, which take place throughout the country. These shows are frequented by chrysanthemum enthusiasts eager to see the prize blooms, the innovations, and to learn how they can improve their own methods of cultivation.

It is difficult to find any plant that has such a long flowering season as the chrysanthemum, with its blooms from August into the New Year, giving the greatest joy during the darkest days of winter. So generously do they display such lovely colours during these months, that horticulturists have devised techniques by which it is possible to grow them during the entire year. Perhaps some purists will view this with disdain, but nobody would deny that to find such a continuous demand for chrysanthemums is an absolute measure of their overwhelming popularity.

Because some readers may become keen competitors at shows, a chapter on exhibiting has been included so that beginners will be able to start on the right lines. Also, for this reason, the classifications and nomenclature used in this book are in accordance with those of the National Chrysanthemum Society. By keeping as close as possible to these the risk of any confusion, which so often arises with plant categories and names, will be avoided. The classification gives the section number followed by 'a' or 'b' according to whether the cultivar is large- or medium-flowered.

The National Chrysanthemum Society (NCS), which came into being in 1846, developed from an association formed by a group of enthusiasts in Stoke Newington. Its activities are devoted to furthering the interest in the growing and exhibition of chrysanthemums. Most local chrysanthemum societies are affiliated to it. Through its influence, uniformity of standards of exhibiting and judging are maintained throughout the country. Some of its more important functions are the examination and assessment of every new cultivar submitted to it, the maintenance of the National Register of Chrysanthemums, the running of annual trials and the publication of a number of authoritative books at very low prices. It organizes two annual national shows—one for early-flowering cultivars in September and another show for the late-flowering cultivars in November.

Membership is open to people interested in chrysanthemums. Among the privileges obtained from membership are the right to exhibit at the Society's shows, free admission to shows and the opportunity to take advantage of the excellent advice that the Society's experts will give on any matters concerning these plants.

A well equipped greenhouse incorporating overhead sprays, immersion-type hot water system, exterior operated roller blinds and sliding sub-stage box ventilations, and removable stage curbing.

THE CHRYSANTHEMUM FAMILY

Although mention of chrysanthemums so often conjures up visions of the enormous blooms often seen at shows, it must be realized, important as these are, that they are only one member of a very large genus. The simple Shasta Daisy or White Marguerite is also a chrysanthemum, the charming yellow Jamaica Primrose is *Chrysanthemum frutescens,* and the correct name for the pyrethrum is *Chrysanthemum coccineum*.

Dealing briefly with the modern cultivated large-flowered exhibition chrysanthemum, which is now known as *C. morifolium*, it is believed to have descended from the oriental plants, *C. sinense*, which has white flowers, and the yellow *C. indicum*. Although chrysanthemums were introduced into Europe late in the 18th century, it was some time afterwards that they reached England. By 1826, there were some fifty varieties being cultivated here. It was the famous plant collector Robert Fortune who was instrumental in the forbears of our modern chrysanthemums being introduced here.

Chrysanthemum sinense, one of the important ancestors of the modern chrysanthemum

Chrysanthemum indicum has also contributed to the development of the modern chrysanthemum. Both are natives of China and southern Japan.

Jamaica Primrose

Chrysanthemum argenteum, grown in a rockery for its silvery foliage

In 1843, he was sent to China by the Royal Horticultural Society. He despatched to England the Chusan Daisy, which was destined to give rise to our present day pompons. Later, from Japan, he dispatched a collection of plants, which led to the large exhibition varieties which are so popular today. At this stage there was a very marked broadening of the colour range available.

Ever since, hybridists have been creating from these rather simple beginnings the masses of far more complicated and superior plants, for which new uses are continuously being found by flower arrangers, florists and gardeners alike.

As mentioned previously, the modern enthusiasm for the beautiful large-flowered varieties has unfortunately tended to obscure the virtues of the many other members of the family, which can be so valuable in the garden. Here they provide continuous colour at a time when the summer flowers are beginning to fade. Although it is not possible to dwell too long on this subject, a few examples are given in the hope that

9

venturesome readers will be inspired to grow some of them.

Chrysanthemum alpinum, picturesquely described as the Marguerite of the Alps, growing only a few inches high, with its white flowers, makes a very attractive carpet in the rockery. Flowering as early as May and June, *C. arcticum,* a 12-inch-high bush gives beautiful lilac-pink flowers. *C. argenteum* provides silvery foliage and for this reason is very valuable. In July, it has wide white flowers on 12-inch stems. Perhaps most charming of all are the cushion chrysanthemums *(C. azaleanum),* which grow as low bushes, 2 to 3 feet high, massed with colourful, semi-double flowers in July and August, creating the illusion that azalea time has come back in the height of summer.

Another species, invaluable in a well-drained rockery, is *C. catanache,* 4 to 6 inches in height, with yellow single flowers with a faint purple ray in spring. The taller varieties *C. erubescens,* which reaches 2 to 2½ feet high, and *C. uliginosum,* with its large white daisy-like flowers towering to a height of 7 feet, are suitable plants for background in a herbaceous border. The real gem

(Left) Pyrethrum
(Below) Chrysanthemum
alpinum

however, planted formally or otherwise, is *C. koreanum*, a species originating from Korea, of which there are many excellent hybrids. These have sprays of both single and double, long-lasting flowers of many hues. Perhaps the most important of all is the species *C. leucanthemum*, a native of Britain, which has pure white single blooms. It is largely to this species that we owe the modern *C. maximum* varieties, such as Esther Read and Wirral Supreme, which play an important part today in the cut-flower industry.

The list is almost inexhaustible, but brief mention must be made of a rare Russian species, *C. macrophyllum*. Silver foliage is the characteristic of *C. mauvii*, which comes from the Atlas Mountains. It has small bright pink flowers which are never absent from the plant from May to October if it is planted in a hot sunny position. It is a lovely plant that should not be overlooked. Finally, another chrysanthemum which has given rise to a large collection of very beautiful single and double cultivars is *C. rubellum*. They are so beautiful and so easy to grow that no garden need be without them.

(Right) Chrysanthemum rubellum
(Below) Chrysanthemum maximum

Modern chrysanthemums

In the previous pages an attempt has been made to draw attention to the broader manifestations of the chrysanthemum family, but undoubtedly the main interest today lies in the more commonly cultivated types, which, it will be appreciated, only represent a section of the whole genus. Even so it is an important one, and a gardener should know the characteristics of the different types that are included in it.

Broadly, chrysanthemums fall into two classes – those that bloom between August and October 1, which are known as early-flowering chrysanthemums, and those flowering from October 1 onwards. The former grow in the open ground during their whole life cycle, whereas the latter are grown mainly in pots, and, although they stand out in the open during the summer, they are brought into the greenhouse to flower so that they are not damaged by frost. These are called late-flowering chrysanthemums.

Although there are other types which will be discussed later, there is no doubt that when most people think of chrysanthemums, they have visions of those impressive large blooms which grace the show bench and are used for decorative purposes on a large scale. Because these are so important some time will be spent giving definitions of the different types that exist.

Exhibition chrysanthemums

Among the late-flowering classes, which bloom indoors during the autumn and winter, are found those enormous spectacular blooms at least 10 inches in diameter. These are now known as large exhibition chrysanthemums. At one time they were called Japanese and incurving Japanese. Among them there are a number of distinct types:

Large exhibition — incurving and reflexing
Medium exhibition — incurving and reflexing
Exhibition incurved

The difference between large and medium is a matter solely of size, mediums being about 8 inches in diameter. The terms incurving, reflexing and incurved are perhaps a little unusual to the newcomer. Although it is important to supplement

Tombola
Early-flowering
intermediate
decorative
NCS Classification
25b

John Woolman
Early-flowering
intermediate
decorative
NCS Classification
25a

Gipsy
Early-flowering
reflexed decorative
NCS Classification
24a

Rayonnante

James Bryant
Late-flowering
large exhibition
NCS Classification 1

(Above) Maylen Late-flowering exhibition incurved
NCS Classification 3b

(Below) Chrysanthemum maximum Variety – Thomas Killan

anything that is said here by seeing the various types at shows and at nurseries, it is hoped that the following definitions will clarify the differences between them.

An *incurving bloom*, which must not be confused with an incurved bloom (to be discussed later), is one in which the florets (commonly and erroneously known as petals) curve inwards towards the centre, forming a globular-shaped flower. These florets are either arranged closely and uniformly, or loosely and irregularly. To be a good bloom, the width must be approximately equal to the depth and be full-centred with florets broad and brilliant in colour.

In *reflexing blooms*, the arrangement of the florets is reversed. They gracefully curve outwards towards the base of the flower. As before, to be perfect the proportions of the width and depth must be equal, the centre well filled and the florets, which may be quilled as well as flat and broad, fresh and bright in colour.

An *exhibition incurved* is a much more rigid affair; its florets, which must be broad, smooth and rounded at the tip, should be long enough to form a graceful curve inwards and be regularly, closely and tightly arranged to form almost a perfect sphere. The flower has the appearance of being a solid mass.

Decorative chrysanthemums
This is a very important class, which has many members with gorgeous and shapely blooms. It contains almost all the

Pompons

Anemones

cultivars grown commercially for cut flowers during the winter. There are both outdoor and indoor varieties.

Early-flowering (outdoor)	Late-flowering (indoor)
Incurved decoratives	Reflexed decoratives
Reflexed decoratives	Intermediate decoratives
Intermediate decoratives	

It is necessary to say at this point that, although the late-flowering types already discussed are known as exhibition chrysanthemums, the decoratives play an equally important part in the show tent. This also applies to a number of the other types to be mentioned later. The blooms of the decoratives are rather smaller than those of the exhibition types. It will be noticed that reflexed and intermediate decoratives appear among both the early and late varieties. They are the same in each case. The perfect reflexed decorative conforms exactly to the standards already laid down for the reflexing form of the large exhibition types. In the intermediate however, more scope is afforded. While being of good proportions, the blooms may incurve, with either closely or regularly arranged florets or ones that are loose and irregular. The intermediate decoratives also include some semi-reflexing, bi-coloured types.

The incurved decoratives, which are exclusive to the early-flowering chrysanthemums, fall very strictly within the definition already given for exhibition incurved cultivars, but they are rather smaller in size.

Charm

Koreans

Anemones

Anemone-centred chrysanthemums are very interesting members of the chrysanthemum family, growing in a wide range of colour, both out of doors and under glass. They are characterized by having a centre which is full of colourful florets instead of an open eye or button as in the ordinary single flower.

Pompons

Perhaps the most versatile variety is the delightfully coloured pompon. There are cultivars for the greenhouse and for the garden. They play an important role in both early and late chrysanthemum shows. No other types can surpass them in their marvellous colour range, which embraces bronze, golden-yellow, white, pink, lilac-rose, crimson, shell-pink, old-gold and many others. Perhaps it is their great variation in dimensions that makes them so attractive. There are dwarfs

Lilian Jackson
Late-flowering single
NCS Classification 7b

Cascade—Niagara

that barely reach 9 inches in height, which can so beautifully adorn rockeries and the front of the border while the taller plants may reach 30 inches. Their blooms, which grow in clusters, always charming, have diameters which range from as little as $\frac{3}{4}$ inch up to 2 inches. Whatever their size, their beautiful pincushion-like blossoms, composed of tightly, regularly arranged florets, never fail to bring joy. They are easy to grow, very accommodating and exceptionally resistant to bad weather.

Singles

From an exhibition point of view, a single chrysanthemum is defined as a bloom with not more than five rows of ray florets emanating from the button centre. There are varieties, suitable for exhibition, decoration, growing in pots and as sprays. They range in height from 18 inches upwards. Their individual blooms can be as small as 3 inches across, while exhibition specimens may be over 5 inches. They have an enormous colour range, embracing almost every colour except blue. The garden cultivars are excellent for mass display.

Korean chrysanthemums

The Korean chrysanthemums are a lovely race of plants, introduced into this country for the first time in 1937. They are mainly grown out of doors, although some are potted for decorations. Grown in the garden they need little more attention than just covering them by heaping up soil or peat around them as protection against frost. Except for the tallest plants, which exceed $2\frac{1}{2}$ feet, no support is necessary. It is difficult to name a class of plants with a more gorgeous range of colour, which includes ox-blood, clear lemon, brick-red, pink-bronze, peach, terracotta and so many more. Their flowers may be either single or double.

In the garden they can be planted in the herbaceous borders, informally mingling with the Michaelmas daisies, both contriving together to prolong the colour well into the autumn. Some gardeners like to put them into formal beds with other plants such as tulips, daffodils, wallflowers, forget-me-nots and summer bedding plants, giving a continuously coloured picture for seven months during the year.

Rayonnantes

Perhaps these are the most intriguing of all chrysanthemums, with their large blooms with spidery petals, embracing a range of lovely colours, including green.

Charm chrysanthemums

Growing as low compact bushes, 2 to 3 feet across and about 18 inches in height, massed with small, single, sweetly scented flowers, they appear rather like Michaelmas daisies. These lovely plants can be cultivated both in the open and in a greenhouse. The present-day varieties include varying shades of red, pink, yellow, bronze and white.

Cascade chrysanthemums

With rather similar flowers to the charm types, cascade chrysanthemums are either grown as bushes in pots, or the pots are placed on a high shelf, allowing their long, flowing, coloured tresses to fall gracefully to the ground. In both cases, it takes a great deal of patient work, training and stopping, to achieve the desired results.

Other types of chrysanthemums

The important *C. maximum* has already been mentioned and will be dealt with in detail later. In addition, note must be taken of the *C. rubellum*, the spray varieties, so valuable for interior decorations, and the spoon chrysanthemums, which are mainly grown out of doors. All have their beauty in colour and form, which cannot be overlooked.

Princess Anne Late-flowering reflexed decorative
NCS Classification 4b

PREPARING TO GROW CHRYSANTHEMUMS

Acquiring a collection

Initially, a large number of gardeners have a few chrysanthemums planted in the garden, perhaps just because a friendly neighbour has given them a root, or they have made a chance purchase on Saturday morning in a local market, or because they are wanted for cut flowers. It could be that a visit to a local show or even the National Chrysanthemum Show may eventually create enthusiasm for these plants.

It is when this interest is aroused that a gardener has to decide what types of chrysanthemums attract him most and how he would like to use them. The type of garden he has, his inclinations, and often those of his wife, are the determining factors. It could be that they like a well laid out garden, massed with colour from early spring to late autumn, supplying flowers and beautiful foliage for flower arrangements. In this case it would be the garden varieties that appeal most, including early-flowering decoratives, outdoor pompons, Korean chrysanthemums, *C. rubellum* and charm varieties.

Another important factor could be the presence of a greenhouse, where the enormous-headed, late-flowering exhibition varieties could be grown.

It is evident that to have a definite plan of work is important when growing chrysanthemums. To devise such a programme it is important to have a clear idea of the uses to which the plants are to be put and the various types available. It is easy enough to grow several groups of plants in the herbaceous borders, but early-flowering chrysanthemums for exhibition need a small piece of ground, where they can flourish without competition from other plants and where proper facilities can be provided for staking them. Late-flowering exhibition types require a greenhouse and an ash-covered base on which to stand the pots during the summer months. For propagating, a cold frame is necessary for both types of chrysanthemums and soil heating equipment is an asset. It will be seen, therefore, that the demands on a small garden, particularly in terms of space, can be quite high.

Charm makes an attractive border.

All beginners have to acquire an initial stock of plants. Sometimes, a friendly enthusiast will give a few cuttings or rooted plants of his favourite varieties. At other times, a neighbour will willingly bestow upon a novice a root of a plant which he wishes to get rid of. Without being ungrateful, the best course for every beginner is to make his own way and acquire his cuttings from a reputable chrysanthemum specialist, who will be overwhelmingly generous with his advice. One important advantage of doing this is that there is a reasonable assurance of avoiding the most prevalent of all chrysanthemum diseases, aspermy virus. This can be eliminated by heat therapy, which is a laboratory technique, that can only be satisfactorily applied by commercial growers.

When buying chrysanthemum cuttings, it must be borne in mind that varieties have their own characteristics – light or dark green leaves, stout or thin stems, varying growth habits, some lanky and others bushy, and so on. If the cuttings are obtained from a reliable source, most of them will thrive. Generally speaking, one would not select long, thin and spindly plants, but it could be that this is their natural growth form and they will do far better ultimately than more robust, stocky, bushy ones of the same variety. This is where the nurseryman can help most, as he knows the plants he is raising and can advise on the best for your purposes.

Foods and fertilizers

In order to flourish chrysanthemums require a suitable environment and proper nutrients in the correct quantities and proportions. A plant's food is produced by its leaves from chemicals derived from the air and soil. The three major parts of the plant concerned with this vitally important operation of manufacturing food are the roots, stems, which act as communication lines and food stores, and the leaves. Thus, it is essential to keep all of them in a good, healthy condition. A plant must have a good root system and strong, green leaves if it is to thrive.

Plants produce their food by a process known as 'photosynthesis'. By this operation, which is carried out mainly in the leaves, they combine carbon dioxide, absorbed from the air, with water sucked up by the roots from the soil, to form starch,

Keystone
Early-flowering
intermediate decorative
NCS Classification 25a

using sunlight as the source of energy for the whole process and chlorophyll, the green substance in the leaves, as a catalyst. From this starch, the essential sugars are produced when required by the plant. It can therefore be seen how vitally important good, clean, healthy foliage, unaffected by disease and uneaten by insects, is to the well-being of a plant. It is, in fact, possible to kill a plant by removing its leaves and thereby starving it. A plant, of course, requires substances other than starch if its life is to be sustained. Once again it is the function of the leaves to make the plant's requirements from the simple chemicals, which have been produced in the soil by the action of bacteria.

It is in this respect that a good root system becomes important. The roots absorb these very important and easily assimilated chemicals, which are conveyed by means of the sap in the stems to the leaves, where they are turned into nutrients in a form that the plant likes. These plant foods are nitrogen, phosphate, potassium, calcium, sulphur, iron and magnesium.

Broadway Early-flowering reflexed decorative NCS Classification 24b

In addition, there are the trace elements manganese, boron, copper and zinc, which are required only in minute quantities, but which are very essential to the well-being of the plant.

As far as chrysanthemums are concerned, the elements required in fairly large quantities are nitrogen, phosphorus and potash, and it is important to ensure that the soil in which they are planted is adequately endowed with them. The best way of doing this is to use a proprietary complete chrysanthemum fertilizer, put down in accordance with the maker's directions. If, however, soil analysis or the condition of the neighbouring plants suggests a shortage of any particular element, a straight fertilizer must be added to the soil to correct any specific defect.

Now what is the function of each of these various elements? The importance of nitrogen is that it stimulates good sturdy growth with very fresh, deep green leaves. For this reason it is essential to apply it early in the season before the buds are formed, to ensure that when they do develop, they will be borne on sturdy plants. It should not, however, be used to excess late in the summer, because then it will encourage soft lush growth which might be subject to 'damping'.

Without adequate supplies of phosphorus, a poor chrysanthemum plant will be grown, because this element is mainly responsible for the formation of a good root system. It is also of great value in strengthening and ripening stalks, enabling them to support the weight of the enormous blooms which are eventually produced on the large exhibition chrysanthemums. Unlike nitrogen, it is important to see that adequate supplies of phosphorus are given when the flowers are being formed. It will result in good, well-formed and intensively coloured blooms.

Potassium has a number of virtues. It plays an essential part in the production of strong green growth, well-ripened wood, resistance to disease and in obtaining flowers of good colour.

Calcium is another element needed by chrysanthemums. When required, it is usually provided by the addition of

Silver Dollar Early-flowering intermediate decorative
NCS Classification 25b

(a) Chlorosis, due to lack of iron, affects younger leaves first. Whole leaf loses colour, whilst older leaves retain dark veins. 'Sequestrene-Plus', 1 oz. per gallon of water, 1 pint per plant is an effective cure.

(b) Potassium deficiency causes yellow edges which spread over whole leaf. The quickest cure is to water the soil with potassium sulphate, 1 tablespoon per gallon of water, 2 gallons per square yard.

(c) Magnesium deficiency affects lower leaves first. Manganese deficiency is almost identical. Spraying with 2 oz. magnesium sulphate with $\frac{1}{2}$ oz. of manganese sulphate in 1 gallon of water cures both troubles.

(d) Healthy leaf. The use of a good general fertilizer, or well rotted farmyard manure, ensures healthy plants.

carbonate of lime. The optimum reaction of the soil for chrysanthemums is a pH value of 6·5. It is only when soil testing shows that the value is appreciably lower than this that lime should be used. Oddly enough, plants do not very often show signs of calcium deficiency. Before the critical level for this disorder is reached, the high acidity of the soil has a detrimental effect and lime has to be added to correct it. Excess lime must be avoided, as it induces chlorosis, shown by a yellowing of the leaves. This is caused by this compound locking-up the supplies of iron and manganese in a form which cannot be assimilated by the plant.

All the elements so far mentioned are needed by the chrysanthemums in fairly large doses. In addition, however, there are a number of others which have to be fed only in minute quantities. For this reason they are known as 'trace' elements. It is sometimes difficult to enumerate specifically the effects of their absence, but whenever there is stunted growth and discoloration and premature fall of the leaves, it might be reasonably suspected that the cause is the lack of one or more of these vital chemicals. Experience has shown that the most likely deficiencies from which chrysanthemums suffer are shortage of boron, manganese, magnesium and iron. Since these elements are required in only minute quantities, it is better to combat any shortage by administering to the soil a general fertilizer containing them all. If the soil or potting compost is fertilized in the manner described in these pages, there is little likelihood of any trouble arising. Garden soil enriched with well-rotted farmyard manure is adequately equipped in this respect.

As mentioned, the most common deficiency disorder which arises from the absence of such elements is chlorosis, due mainly to the lack of iron and manganese, particularly in an alkaline soil (a chalky or well-limed one), where this disorder is rife. The best remedy is to water the ground with a suspension of Sequestrene-Plus in water, in accordance with the maker's instructions.

As previously mentioned, it usually pays the amateur to apply a proprietary general chrysanthemum fertilizer, because the quantities of the 'trace' elements required are so small that they are difficult to weigh out and to incorporate evenly into

Sources of nitrogen

Fertilizer	Per cent nitrogen	Other particulars
Organic		
Dried blood	7 to 14	Fairly quick acting.
Hoof and horn meal	7 to 15	Fairly quick acting.
Meat and bone meal	4 to 5	16 – 20 per cent phosphate.
Fishmeal	5 to 10	6 – 14 per cent phosphate.
Soot	2 to 7	6 – 14 per cent phosphate.
Inorganic		
Ammonium nitrate	35	Very soluble and quick acting.
Ammonium sulphate	21	If applied in solution does not scorch.
Sodium nitrate	16	Acts immediately.

Sources of phosphate

Fertilizer	Per cent phosphate	Other particulars
Organic		
Bone meal	22	3·5 per cent nitrogen. Slow acting.
Steamed bone meal	29	Faster acting than bone meal.
Inorganic		
Superphosphate	19	Portion acts quickly: rest slowly. Rate enhanced by incorporating with ammonium sulphate.

Photosynthesis

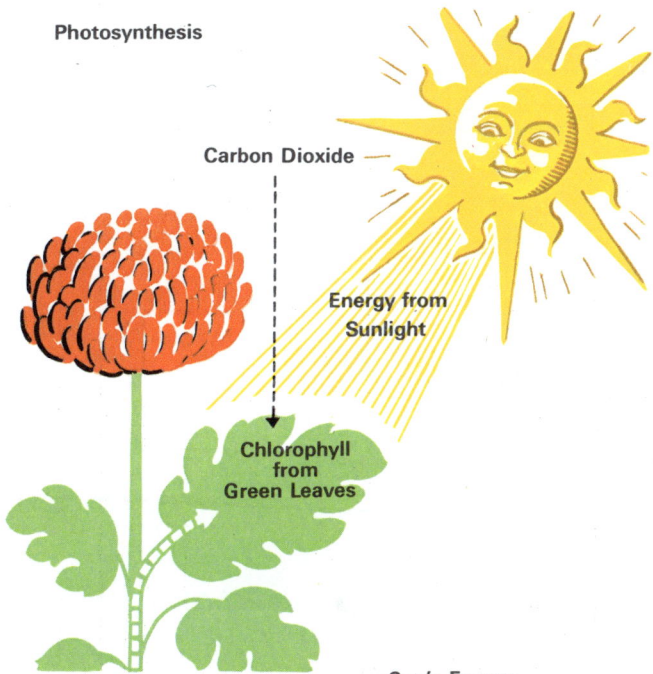

Carbon Dioxide

Energy from Sunlight

Chlorophyll from Green Leaves

Carbon Dioxide + Water
(From Air)   (From Soil)

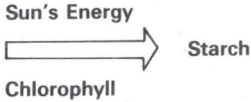

Sun's Energy

Chlorophyll

Starch

Water

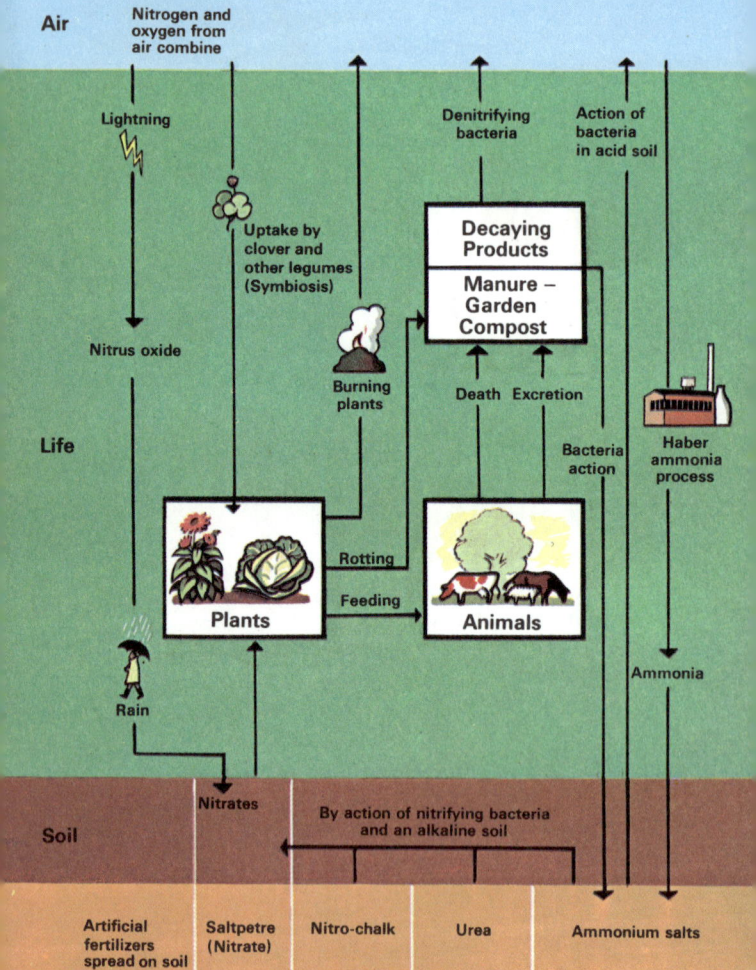

The Nitrogen Cycle
Nitrogen in air

Air

Nitrogen and oxygen from air combine

Lightning

Nitrus oxide

Uptake by clover and other legumes (Symbiosis)

Denitrifying bacteria

Action of bacteria in acid soil

Decaying Products

Manure – Garden Compost

Burning plants

Death   Excretion

Bacteria action

Haber ammonia process

Life

Rotting

Feeding

Plants

Animals

Rain

Ammonia

Nitrates

Soil

By action of nitrifying bacteria and an alkaline soil

Artificial fertilizers spread on soil

Saltpetre (Nitrate)

Nitro-chalk

Urea

Ammonium salts

Sources of potash

Fertilizer	Per cent potash	Other particulars
Organic		
Wood ash	10 to 15	Acts immediately. Should be kept dry.
Inorganic		
Potassium sulphate	50	Acts quickly. Lasts in the soil. Does not burn roots.
Potassium nitrate	46	15 per cent nitrogen. Quick acting.

Sources of all three nutrients

Fertilizer	Per cent nitrogen (approx.)	Per cent phosphate (approx.)	Per cent potash (approx.)
Farmyard manure	2·0	1·0	1·5 to 3·0
Poultry manure, raw	3·0 to 6·0	3·5	1·5 to 2·0
deep litter	3·0	3·0 to 7·0	2·0
Garden compost	2·0	0·5	0·5 to 2·0
Spent hops	3·5	1·5	trace
Activated secondary sewage sludge	5·0	3·5	0·5

the bulk of the mixture.

A chrysanthemum grower, nevertheless, should know the sources of the various chemicals needed, because an occasion might arise when one particular element is needed. The requirements of these plants can be supplied by either organic fertilizers or inorganic chemicals. The advantage of the inorganics is that they act quickly, as they are simple compounds which have not to be decomposed to turn them into substances in a form that the plant can absorb. Although some people adhere strictly to the belief that organic fertilizers give the best results, there is no evidence to support this view. Artificial feeds are equally good and are usually cheaper. There is, however, one very striking advantage in using organic fertilizers such as farmyard manure, sewage compost and spent hops, in that they provide ample quantities of humus, which is essential to the good cultivation of chrysanthemums. They revel in soil rich in humus, which imparts to it exceptional moisture retentive powers and a plentiful supply of nitrogenous material, which slowly decomposes and provides nitrogen over a long period. As a guide details of the sources of the most important nutrients are shown on pages 30 and 33.

Preparing fibrous loam from turfs. A stack is made with strawy-manure and lime in layers between the turfs.

Potting composts

Because indoor varieties, in most instances, spend the whole of their life in pots it is necessary to provide the correct potting soil or compost. It is important that this compost is not confused with garden compost, which is prepared by rotting down organic material. Potting composts are composed of carefully mixed fibrous loam, peat and sand, to which fertilizers are added. In more recent years, horticulturists have developed another growing medium for pot plants. This is soilless compost, which will be discussed later.

Essentially, compost for chrysanthemums should be composed of the ingedients mentioned above. To be of the right quality, it is important that they should meet certain well-defined specifications. The loam should be sufficiently fibrous. This is best prepared from decomposed turfs. Ordinary garden soil does not contain enough fibre. Ideally this loam should be slightly acid, with a pH value of 6·5. In former days, it was the practice of chrysanthemum enthusiasts to prepare loam by stacking freshly cut, pasture-land turfs. Today, however, the range of John Innes composts which are available have largely eliminated this arduous task.

Stack with air spaces between the turfs and cover with a polythene sheet as shown.

Peat is an important ingredient of potting composts. Leaf-mould may be used in its place, but it should be remembered that it contains pests, disease and harmful bacteria, which necessitates sterilization. On the other hand, peat is sterile and rarely contaminated. Most authorities claim that sedge peat is the best and it is worth noting that the British Standards Institution has recently published a specification (BSS 4156) for peat. This permits it to be marketed under the Institution's Kite Mark, which undoubtedly is a guarantee of high quality.

Sand is an essential ingredient of any compost intended for chrysanthemum growing. It has the particular quality of encouraging the development of the root system. Such material should be coarse and sharp so that it enables the soil surface in the pots or trays to keep free from caking and to be well open or friable, particularly at the time when cuttings are being rooted. It is recommended that when buying sand for this purpose, a gardener should see that it is washed and sharp, and is graded between very fine and one-eighth of an inch.

John Innes potting composts

After much research work at the John Innes Horticultural Institution, various grades of John Innes Potting Compost have been developed. The table on pages 38 and 39 gives the formulae of the four John Innes composts used in the cultivation of chrysanthemums. The differences between the grades is in the increasing amounts of base feed and ground chalk added to the other ingredients.

Unfortunately, the formulae which are given, and which are commonly used, are expressed in a mixed bag of units, which often causes difficulty with the amateur. Some ingredients are measured by weights (pounds and ounces) and others by volumes (bushels). In order to clarify the position the data on pages 38 and 39 may be helpful.

Sometimes granulated charcoal (as lumps up to $\frac{1}{4}$ inch) is mixed with the compost because of its great absorption powers for gases. This helps to keep the soil sweet by removing any toxic gases arising from decomposition, and thus contributes materially to the maintenance of a healthy root system.

Before leaving this subject, it must be mentioned that after the rooting stage, for which John Innes No. 1 compost is

The Carbon Cycle

Carbon dioxide in the air (0 · 03%)

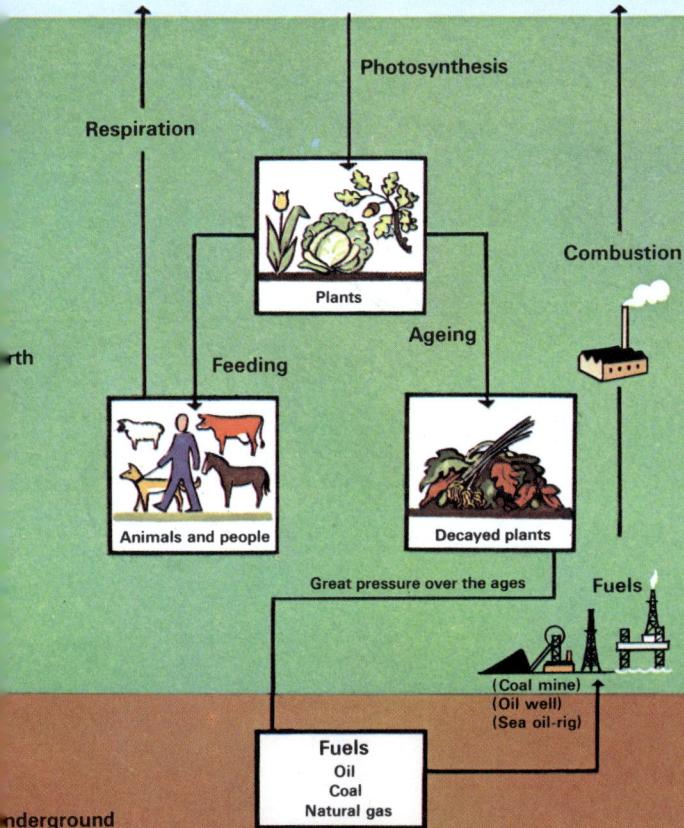

Respiration

Photosynthesis

Combustion

Plants

Feeding

Ageing

Animals and people

Decayed plants

rth

Great pressure over the ages

Fuels

(Coal mine)
(Oil well)
(Sea oil-rig)

Fuels
Oil
Coal
Natural gas

nderground

rbon dioxide from the air is absorbed by plants to form foods through the process
photosynthesis. Animals, including humans, eat these plants and breathe out
rbon dioxide. Dead plants and animals are for years subjected to high under-
ound pressure and many centuries later yield fuels which when burnt return
rbon dioxide to the atmosphere.

John Innes Potting Composts

No. 1

Fibrous loam	7 bushels
Horticultural peat	3 bushels
Coarse sand	2 bushels
Ground chalk or limestone	9 ozs
John Innes base feed	2 lbs 13 ozs

Use in chrysanthemum growing

For rooting cuttings in beds or boxes

The formula of John Innes base feed is:

Potting soil measures

1 cwt of potting soil = approx 1¼ bushels

One bushel fills a box of 22 in × 10 in × 10 in,

or six standard seed boxes 14 in × 8½ in filled 3 in deep

No. 2	No. 3	No. 4
7 bushels	7 bushels	7 bushels
3 bushels	3 bushels	3 bushels
2 bushels	2 bushels	2 bushels
1 lb 2 ozs	1 lb 11 ozs	2 lbs 4 ozs
5 lbs 10 ozs	8 lbs 7 ozs	11 lbs 4 ozs
For the first transplanting of rooted cuttings into $3\frac{1}{2}$-inch pots	For plants moved to 5 to 6-inch pots	For final potting into 8 to 10-inch pots, in which the plants flower

2 parts by weight hoof and horn meal
2 parts by weight superphosphate of lime
1 part by weight sulphate of potash

Compost measures for potting on

1 cwt is enough for: 112 rooted cuttings planted into 3-inch pots (sixties)

transplanting 62 plants from 3-inch pots to $4\frac{1}{2}$-inch pots (forty-eights)

transplanting 20 plants from $4\frac{1}{2}$-inch pots to 8-inch pots (twenty-fours)

Early flowering variety after blooming before being cut down.

invariably used, satisfactory results have been obtained by chrysanthemum experts, using a mixture of eight bushels fibrous loam, two and a half bushels moist horticultural peat and one and a half bushels of dry, coarse sand to which are added the appropriate amount of fertilizers.

Soilless composts

Soilless composts have been developed in quite recent times. There is no doubt that the best medium for growing chrysanthemums is John Innes compost, but because of an increasing shortage of good top soil it is difficult to maintain a high standard. In consequence, soilless composts, which are composed of peat and washed sand in equal proportions, have been developed. They are far better than inferior quality John Innes composts. There is one formula containing sand and peat together with potassium nitrate, superphosphate, dolomite lime and calcium carbonate lime which is used solely for striking cuttings, while a second, which contains, in addition, hoof and horn meal, is used for rooted cuttings and growing on.

After-care of stools

After a gardener has bought his first collection of chrysanthemums, it is the practice to propagate new stock every season. The principal and most simple way of doing this is by rooting cuttings taken from the root stocks, which are called stools, of the plants that have flowered during the previous season.

It will be realized that since the plants that are to be grown in the following season depend upon them, it is vitally important that every attention is given to them after they have finished flowering. It is so important that this point in time may be regarded as the start of the chrysanthemum grower's year. When all the blooms have faded, the first thing to do is to look at each one very critically and decide whether it is in a strong, healthy condition. In fact, this review should commence rather earlier during the season; notes should be made of the really good flowers and plants. It is impossible to over-emphasize the importance of this procedure, because carelessness will lead to seriously deteriorated stock. Plants that do not meet the high standard should be dug up and burnt.

When flowering has finished, the selected plants of the early-flowering chrysanthemums are cut down to about 6 to 9 inches from the ground, so that all the soft growth and large leaves are removed, leaving the hardened stalks. Before the ground becomes too wet the stools should be lifted. This is probably best done in early November. Although it is not practised by all gardeners, it has been found that washing the stools with running water to clear off all the soil is beneficial. It certainly removes the slugs.

After the water has drained off they are packed in boxes, lightly covered with compost and stored in a cold frame. Alternatively, they can be planted in beds in a cold greenhouse. A very good method is to cover up to five stools with

A lifted stool should first be inspected for damage or disease; diseased stools should be burned.

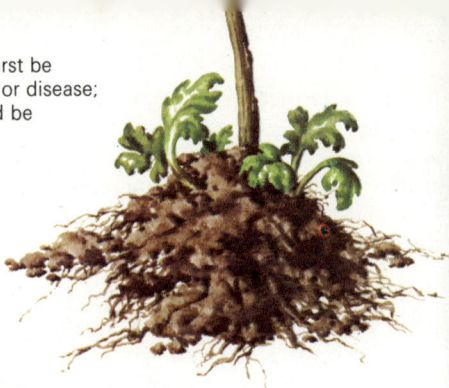

Stool washed and trimmed — note coarse basal growth removed. The stool, when dry, should be sprinkled with lime or flowers of sulphur.

soil in a large plastic pot. This number is usually as many of any one variety that an amateur requires. The great advantage of this procedure lies in the ease of handling.

Stools of indoor varieties are similarly cut down to 6 to 9 inches, but they are not removed from their pots. In their particular case, there must be no delay in cutting plants down after flowering because the interval until the new cuttings are required is very short. They are then kept in a light and airy position in the greenhouse.

The stools do not require much water for several months; only sufficient should be given initially to settle the compost around the roots. It is important that the stools are clearly labelled when cut down.

During the resting period, the stools should not be subjected to high temperature – never higher than 50°F. There are some varieties, of which the October-flowering President is an example, which tend to produce rosettes of leaves instead of flowering stems at the base of the stools. Exposure to high temperatures during the winter prompts this. Such chrysanthemums benefit if their stools or rooted cuttings are maintained for three weeks at a temperature not exceeding 40°F. This treatment is known as *vernalization*.

42

PROPAGATION

There are three ways of propagating chrysanthemums – by seeds, division of roots, and cuttings. The best way is by cuttings. The main objection to growing from seeds is that seedlings seldom develop true to type. The drawback with the division method is that it allows diseases to be readily carried over from one season to another.

The method of taking cuttings is the same for all types of chrysanthemums, but the time of rooting varies with the variety and depends to some extent on the period required to reach maturity and the subsequent treatment they need to reach perfection. In this respect, nothing can be better than to quote the recommendations made by the National Chrysanthemum Society, membership of which is worth the while of all enthusiasts:

Type	Date to take cuttings
Varieties to produce large specimen plants	November
Large exhibition varieties	December and January
Exhibition incurved	January and early February
Decoratives, late-flowering singles and pompons	Late January and February
Early-flowering varieties (outdoor)	Mid February and March
Decoratives for dwarf plants	April and early May

Depending on the primary object of growing the plants, these dates might be slightly altered. It has been found by some chrysanthemum growers that if the date of taking cuttings of some of the outdoor varieties is advanced to early February, it is possible to 'stop' the plants twice, once in March and again in April. By this means, five or six flowering stems are produced with no deleterious effect in the quality of the blooms. For those growing for cut flowers, this is a useful procedure.

There are two types of gardeners interested in growing chrysanthemums – those who have a greenhouse and those who have not. In the case of the former, the propagation of chrysanthemums presents no difficulty, but it is rather harder and slower for the latter. Nevertheless, it can be done success-fully. It is, however, essential to have a garden frame. If it has plastic soil-heating cables, so much the better.

Probably the most frequent cause of failure to root cuttings is taking them from stems which have not sprung into life after their long resting period. The cuttings must be growing healthily when they are taken, otherwise they will not root and grow. Although it entails a little more trouble, heat un-doubtedly helps the stools to burst into active growth at the required time.

At one time, the only way of heating the greenhouse was by means of a solid-fuel boiler or an electrical heating apparatus. Obviously, it was a very uneconomic practice to heat the entire greenhouse. Nowadays, plastic covered heating cables, on which boxes of stools can be placed, will cheaply bring the

Plants placed in the greenhouse should not be overcrowded, in order that the air can circulate freely.

stools to life. The owner of a large greenhouse can install soil warming cables under the stool-beds, supplied with electricity from the mains through a transformer. This will provide sufficient heat to start the stools growing. An amateur, who does not have a greenhouse, can get his stools started easily and his cuttings rooted quite successfully if he installs a plastic-covered soil heating cable in the bed of a frame. However, because such heating will have little effect on the surrounding air, the procedure will take rather longer than in a greenhouse. Without a greenhouse, of course, it will only be possible to grow early-flowering chrysanthemums.

Taking cuttings

It is usual to take cuttings from the base of the old stools and these are better than those which grow from the stem. It is, however, not absolutely necessary and

(a) This enlarged illustration of a cutting shows which leaves are to be carefully removed (x). Until roots are formed, cuttings must exist on sap in the leaves and stem. Therefore, defoliation must not be too drastic. Three cuttings: *(b)* correct, *(c)* over-developed, *(d)* too coarse.

Taking a basal cutting when stools show vigorous growth.

(a) Stem cutting with a 'heel'. They are taken when the plant is 'shy' to grow basal shoots.
(b) Basal cutting is trimmed just below a node.

sometimes circumstances dictate that they must be stem cuttings, which are the side shoots. It is important to ensure that there is good healthy growth on the stools at the time of taking the cuttings, and that this has been produced after the stools have had a long resting period during the winter. Good cuttings are healthy and neither sappy nor hard. They should have short spaces between the leaf joints. Also, they should not be too thick, ideally with stems about $\frac{1}{8}$ inch in diameter, with four or five, fresh firm leaves. It helps to water the stools the day before severing the cuttings from them. In this condition, it will be possible to make a clean cut. To prevent the cuttings becoming infested with aphids, it is as well to spray the stools thoroughly with an insecticide such as B.H.C. or Malathion.

Root cuttings are taken by severing the basal shoots just below a joint (node) with a sharp knife. The base of each cutting should be cut cleanly without ragged edges. It may also be necessary to trim off one or two lower leaves to give a clear stem for insertion in the compost. Stem cuttings are obtained by gently tearing off the side shoots when 1 or 2 inches long from the main stem, with a heel of the old wood. Normally the cuttings root readily without the aid of rooting compounds, but quicker rooting and much larger root systems can be induced by treating them with a hormone rooting preparation. This is a simple process, consisting of dipping the end of the stem into water, then into the rooting compound, tapping off surplus powder and inserting it into the compost. Do not allow the cut-off shoots to stand in water for any length of time, as is done with hard wood stems, as the excess water absorbed is likely to induce rotting and consequent failure. The cuttings are spaced round the edge of a $3\frac{1}{2}$ inch pot about $1\frac{1}{2}$ inches apart in holes about 1 inch deep made with a thin bamboo cane or a pencil. Seed boxes may also be used, in which case space the cuttings 2 inches apart in four rows across the width of the box,

The cuttings, moistened with water, are dipped in rooting powder and planted around the edge of the pot about $1\frac{1}{2}$ inches apart. The soil is then covered with a layer of sand.

Cuttings are planted in rows 4 inches apart.

so that it holds twenty-four plants. The planting medium in both cases should be moist, but not wet, John Innes Potting Compost No. 1.

Place a thin layer of dry coarse sand on the surface of the compost so that when the hole is made some falls to the bottom. The lower end of each cutting then rests on a little sand, which assists root formation and provides drainage. After cuttings have been gently firmed, water well, using a fine-rosed watering can. The boxes and pots should be immediately labelled. There is little to choose between pots and boxes, but the former normally dry out more rapidly and need more watering. Some growers, however, claim that cuttings in pots root quicker than those in boxes.

The boxes or pots are then placed in a warm, close atmosphere until the cuttings root and show signs of growing. If the compost is initially made sufficiently moist, there is little need to add further water. Over watering will soon cause the cuttings to rot.

Sometimes, because of the callus tissue which is formed as a thick skin at the bottom of the stems, the cuttings flag prior to the formation of roots. This should be remedied by spraying or sprinkling them overhead with water. On bright days, it is necessary to give them shade, particularly during the first few days. Covering them with sheets of newspaper is quite effective for this purpose. Care should, however, be taken not to prolong this practice, otherwise blanched weak growth will form.

Ideally, the cuttings should be kept at a temperature of 60°F, in soil at 65°F. As soon as they become robust in appearance, showing that they have rooted, ventilation should be given and the temperature lowered to 45°F. This ensures that a good root system is developed and the strength is diverted from providing excess top growth. This should be done by trans-

Cuttings placed under glass soon take root.

When cuttings have developed to this stage they are potted in 3″ pots.

These two well-rooted cuttings
will now need a larger pot.
On sunny days cuttings should
be protected with paper.

ferring the young plants to a cooler part of the greenhouse or a cooler frame. A sudden drop in temperature is likely to cause the skin on the undersides of the leaves to separate. Eventually, a dead black patch develops.

Following this, the next stage depends upon whether the chrysanthemums are outdoor or indoor varieties. For outdoor plants, as soon as they are used to cooler conditions the cuttings are transferred to a cold frame, where they remain until the middle of March. They are transplanted to a frame bed, formed of a layer of consolidated ashes on which is placed 2 inches of John Innes Potting Compost No. 2. This keeps their roots compact. So that the young plants develop strongly, they need to be planted 4 inches apart. Alternatively, they can be planted into boxes and placed in a cold frame.

With late-flowering varieties, the rooted cuttings are planted directly into small (3-inch) pots and placed in a frame. Chrysanthemums required primarily for decorative purposes can be placed in a cold frame in much the same way as described for the early-flowering varieties. Subsequently they are planted

Polythene bags can be used to strike a small number of cuttings. As they grow the bag will need support.

into 8 or 9-inch pots at the end of May, by which time they should have a good root system, at least forming a 4-inch cube in size. To minimize labour costs, frequently commercial growers do not pot their chrysanthemums on. For plants destined to produce exhibition blooms, it is usual to transplant the rooted cuttings into a series of pots of increasing size in the manner to be described later.

After the chrysanthemums have been put into frames, which are kept closed for a few days to encourage root action, they are left without watering for at least a week or ten days, except for a light overhead spraying just after planting. Even after this, the plants should be watered moderately. From this point onwards, it is the objective to produce sturdy plants. Increased ventilation should be given by adjusting the frame-lights, until about the end of April, when the plants will be completely hardy. After this, the frame-lights are left off, except during heavy rain storms or under frosty conditions.

Rooting a small number of cuttings

There are several methods by which an amateur without a frame or a greenhouse can root a small number of cuttings. In one such method, a sheet of polythene, about 8 inches wide and 18 to 20 inches long, is spread out on a table. On this is flattened out a mixture of moist peat and sand to form a 2-inch wide strip, about $\frac{1}{2}$ to $\frac{3}{4}$ inches deep, so that one of its lengthwise edges is about 3 inches from that of the polythene. The cuttings are then laid on it, about $2\frac{1}{2}$ inches apart with their ends inserted into the compost. The polythene is folded up over the cuttings and the ends tucked in and the whole packet carefully rolled into a bundle and secured with a rubber band. This is then kept in a warm corner – on a window-sill, for example – and the cuttings will be seen to root in about three weeks.

Cuttings can also be successfully rooted in pots or seed pans completely enclosed in a polythene bag, keeping them in a warm, light place. To prevent the bag touching the plants, small sticks should be inserted into the soil. The humid conditions created inside the polythene bag are ideal for striking cuttings.

STOPPING, TIMING, SECURING AND DISBUDDING

To most people the above terminology may be bewildering, but as the terms represent only simple operations the beginner should not be put off.

A chrysanthemum cultivar (variety) left to its own devices would produce many shoots and a wealth of blooms, but they would be very small and often unattractive. Even if it is the object to grow chrysanthemums for garden display, it is necessary to restrict excessive growth. Early-flowering chrysanthemums can develop splendid flowers if grown with moderate control in garden borders. For cut flower and exhibition purposes, restriction in the number of blooms per plant becomes of paramount importance, because it has direct bearing on their quality.

Exhibitors of chrysanthemums who have specified show dates on which to produce flowers can, within certain limits, control the time of blooming.

When rooted cuttings are allowed to grow they develop a main stem, with leaves growing at intervals on either side. A flower bud is produced at its tip. When this bud reaches a

certain stage, side shoots appear at the leaf axils, which are the spaces between the leaves and the stalk, where they join. These shoots are termed breaks or lateral growths and the bud is called a break bud. If break buds are allowed to remain they either die or produce only very poor flowers. As soon as break buds appear, it is the practice to remove them.

In turn each of these breaks will develop a bud at its tip, which is known as a 'first-crown bud'. This will, in most cases, grow and produce a first quality flower. Most early-flowering chrysanthemums flower on first-crown buds. There are, however, instances where it is not always desirable to accept this bud. Examples are late-flowering varieties, where this bloom is likely to be poor in colour or the florets so tightly packed that the flower is mis-shaped. Often, cut-flower growers discard this bud so as to increase the number of blooms produced on each plant. In such cases, the first-crown bud is removed to allow others to grow on a number of the side shoots. A bud so produced is called a 'second-crown bud'. This rather simple action is called by chrysanthemum experts 'running on'. It is a very useful method to adopt when the first-crown bud is damaged, on a too short stem or when it comes too early to make a show date.

(a) Rooted cutting. (b) Cutting develops a main stem with leaves at intervals along its length. (c) Growing naturally a bud appears at the top. When this is partially developed 'lateral growths' or 'breaks' grow from 'leaf axils'. This bud either flowers poorly or dies. For good plants this bud-producing tip is removed when the breaks first appear.

A break which is already formed, in the manner described, before the break bud has been removed is known as a natural break.

'Stopping' is the removal of the top $\frac{1}{2}$-inch of the main stem before the break bud appears, breaking it off, not pinching it out, without taking away any fully developed leaves. By this action, side shoots will be encouraged to grow earlier than they would if left to develop naturally. This is mainly done to control the time of blooming, because in many varieties to wait for the natural break might mean extremely late flowers.

Most of the early-flowering chrysanthemums give their best blooms from first-crown buds, produced in the majority of cases after stopping on specific dates. The dates have been worked out by experts and this information is usually available from chrysanthemum nurserymen. In addition, the Chrysanthemum Society publishes comprehensive stopping and timing tables. The practice of stopping and timing is fairly simple for early-flowering varieties, particularly the decoratives.

Late-flowering chrysanthemums are more intricate. Both exhibitors and cut-flower growers wish to control the

Young plants before formation of break bud. Lateral growths developing. Arrows indicate shoots which could be used should crown bud be damaged or fail to develop well.

Plant stopped by removal of entire leaf cluster. Note young laterals appearing in leaf axils.

First crown buds developed, which should be secured by removing shoots at all leaf axils and secondary buds.

(a) Second stopping by removal of first break to produce second crown buds. Dark green shoot grows to develop second crown buds which are secured as previously described.

(b) 'Running on'. The first crown bud is rubbed out *after* it has formed. This process is used when the bud has formed too early for the show, or has been damaged. It is also useful when a variety flowers best on second crown buds.

number and quality of their blooms and also to regulate the time of flowering. Among the ways to achieve the latter are adjusting the time when the cuttings are rooted, and selecting the breaks to be allowed to develop. Usually those lower down the stem are later and longer in length than the others. Removing selected breaks is also a way of controlling the number of flowers produced. The chrysanthemum grower's parlance for this procedure is 'counting down'. An exhibitor requiring only three or four first-class blooms counts down to this number, whereas a market grower would let eight or nine breaks develop.

Once this number has been determined, it is necessary to 'disbud' by removing every unwanted lateral shoot and bud on a stem to allow the selected one to grow to its fullest extent. This action is described as 'securing a bud'.

Finally, a bud is sometimes surrounded by other flower buds. This marks the end of further vegetative growth of the plant and is called a 'terminal bud'. The surplus buds are removed, leaving the central one. In some varieties the second-crown bud is the terminal bud.

CULTIVATING EARLY-FLOWERING VARIETIES

These cultivars are largely grown for exhibition and cutting, but they can be grown in borders, where they give a delightful display of colour in late summer and autumn.

Choice and preparation of site

Early-flowering chrysanthemums are not difficult to grow. However, the correct choice of a site well suited to the needs of the variety grown is quite important if the best results are to be obtained. It is also important not to risk exposing them to severe frost. If your garden is in a frost pocket, it might be as well to abandon any idea of growing them in the open and to erect a greenhouse and grow, instead, late-flowering cultivars.

The ground must be well-drained, because chrysanthemums loathe being waterlogged. They are surface-rooting and normally do not need deep tillage. If drainage is not good, double dig and break up the subsoil to make it more permeable. Finally, the site should be sunny and sheltered from the wind.

Although chrysanthemums hate being waterlogged, they revel in an abundance of humus in the soil, because in addition to its water-retaining properties it opens up the soil and leads to a good root system.

Moisture retained by humus provides water, which is much needed by heavily leafed plants in the warmer months. Farmyard manure, horse or cow, is ideal; preferably not pig because it is wet and cold and does not decompose so readily. Unfortunately, manure is a rare commodity these days.

It is often necessary to substitute for these materials spent hops, sewage sludge composted with straw, peat mixed with bonemeal, or poultry manure, which has been stacked for some months between layers of soil. Careful preparation of the site is essential during the winter, well ahead of planting time, putting the manure in fairly deeply. If it is not possible to dig the bed until spring, good results can be obtained by incorporating John Innes Base Fertilizer or a proprietary mixture, specially blended for chrysanthemums.

Chrysanthemums dislike very acid soil. Soil acidity is measured by a scale of pH values – a low figure of 4·0 indicates high acidity, a high value like 8·0 great alkalinity. Chrysanthemums prefer the pH to be about 6·5, which is slightly on the acid side of neutral. Normally, incorporating $\frac{1}{4}$ ounce of carbonate of lime or ground chalk in each square yard renders the soil suitable. However, if it is suspected that the soil is acid, it is advisable to test for pH value, using one of the kits which are now on the market. If the result is only slightly below 6·5 the dose of carbonate of lime might be effectively increased to $\frac{1}{2}$ ounce to each square yard. If, however, the pH value is found to be very low, it would be as well to consult the local county horticultural adviser, who would advise on the best treatment. The quantity of carbonate of lime that is likely to be added would adequately protect the plants against calcium deficiency.

The best time for planting out early-flowering chrysanthemums is between the middle and end of May, unless a late frost is expected, when it should be postponed. Dry and friable soil is best. On no account must it be wet and soggy. When early flowering chrysanthemums are grown for exhibition and cutting, as is often the case, they are more manageable if grown in rows in a plot, specially set aside for the purpose. Plant them 18 inches apart, with 21 inches between each row and a 30 inch path between every three or four rows, according to their ultimate size. If there are a large number of plants, and there is space to spare, it is a good thing to adopt the system used by commercial growers, who put their plants 15 inches apart, with 15 inches between the rows and a 3-foot path every three rows. The advantage of this method is that it permits the use of standard frame lights to be erected as a shield against frost and heavy rain.

When transplanting, do not damage the roots. If the cuttings have been grown in a frame bed, they should be healthy and strong, and little difficulty should be experienced.

Irrespective of whether the rooted cuttings are in pots, boxes or frames, they should be given a good soaking of water. When planted in the ground, the roots must be well firmed with saucer-shaped hollows left around each stem to trap water. These also afford some protection to the small plants against strong winds. If they have been well watered beforehand, there is little need for any more for some time, although overhead spraying once a week or so will freshen the leaves.

Materials needed to test, and if necessary, adjust pH value of soil; distilled water, test tablets, ground chalk or carbonate of lime, peat and soil.

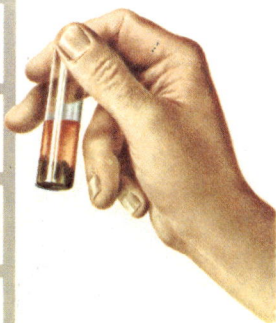

Use lime	**Strongly acid**
Lime advisable	**Acid**
Soil correct	**Slightly acid**
Do not use lime use peat	**Alkaline**

Test soil, taken from top 3", is thoroughly mixed. As it may vary in different areas of the garden, test where plants are to grow.

a

b

62

c

(a) Leslie Thomas
Early-flowering
reflexed decorative
NCS Classification 24b
(b) Tracey Waller
Early-flowering
reflexed decorative
NCS Classification 24a
(c) Graham Knight
Early-flowering
intermediate decorative
NCS Classification 25b
(d) Joe Edwards
Early-flowering
intermediate decorative
NCS Classification 25a

d

This procedure will encourage the roots to grow vigorously in their new surroundings.

Staking is very important, both with early and late-flowering chrysanthemums. The method adopted depends to a certain extent upon the number of plants grown. Wherever possible, provide a stake for each plant and one for each bloom. It is best to put the main stakes in the ground at the intended spacings of the plants, then planting at a later date the plants in position. This is better than planting and staking at the same time. If space permits, wires can be fixed to posts at either end of each row. Bamboo canes, which are used for the individual staking, can be each tied to the wires as they are put into position. It is very important to ensure that the plants are securely tied to the stakes. Three-ply fillis is better than raffia, but many gardeners are using paper-covered wire ties for a first tie, which must be low down on the stem.

As the plants grow, more ties must be fixed higher up the stem. Much of the success in growing chrysanthemums lies in

Two earlies showing good root.

Planting out against a stake.

Soil should be made firm around the root.

After tying plant to stake a depression should be made in the soil for watering.

Two methods of making rows. *(Left)* Three rows 21 inches apart with a 30-inch path. *(Right)* Commercial method, three rows 15 inches apart with a 30-inch path

diligently carrying out this task. With fillis or raffia, a tie should be first made tightly round the stake and then loosely round the stem to allow for growth.

When a moderately large number of chrysanthemums are grown, either outdoors or indoors, the use of 8-inch, 13-gauge, 'Weldmesh' supports is recommended. It is sold commercially in rolls, 30 feet long by 40 inches wide. At the end of each season the rolls can be rolled up and stowed away. One method in which it can be erected is by driving into the ground, at each end of the bed, two posts about 32 to 34 inches apart. A length of angle iron or gas piping is firmly fixed to the outside wire of the roll at each end. Initially, when planting, the mesh is kept at ground level, acting as a planting guide. The mesh is then raised and fixed on the end posts some inches above the ground. Each plant is thus adequately supported. As the plants grow, the mesh is raised, always maintaining it about 12 inches below the tops of the plants. Sagging in the middle of the mesh is prevented by tying it to bamboo canes at either side at various points along its length.

Maintenance

In the early days, the beds should be regularly hoed to maintain the top 2-inch layer of soil in a fine, soft condition. At all times, hoeing should not be carried out close to the plants, as surface roots are likely to be damaged. This is particularly important later in the summer, when the plants are large. In any case, while hoeing keeps the ground free of weeds in the initial stages, by the summer the plants will have grown to such an extent that the weeds will be smothered. In addition, summer mulching will prevent their growth.

If hoeing is done initially, and provided the roots are well-watered before transplantation, the plants will need only little water for some weeks, except in a drought. If watering becomes necessary, the ground must be completely saturated.

Overhead spraying is particularly beneficial in warm weather, especially if it is done with a sprinkler which gives a

'Weldmesh' method of staking. Netting is raised as plants develop.

fine mist. It must, however, be remembered that at no time after the buds are showing colour must overhead watering be carried out, as the flowers might then be blemished.

Using a hoe is an excellent method of weeding. Commercial horticulturalists, however, use chemical weedkillers which save them a considerable amount of labour. For the amateur, there are two types of weedkillers which would serve this purpose. The first is based on paraquat and has to be watered on to the leaves of the weeds during the summer. It is usually applied by means of a specially designed bar attachment to an ordinary watering can. The other type of weedkiller has simazine as its active ingredient. This prevents the germination of the weed seeds. It needs to be applied to the soil in the winter and once it is put down, the soil must be left undisturbed during the rest of the summer.

Feeding

Improved colour and larger blooms can be obtained by giving chrysanthemums liquid manure feeds during the growing

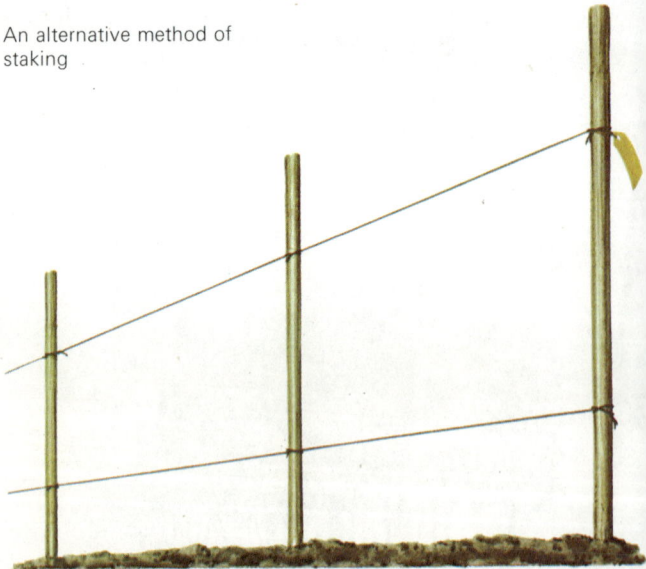

An alternative method of staking

season. To get initial rapid growth early in the year, they require nitrogen, which is best supplied by watering the soil with either a solution of urea (1 ounce to 6 gallons water), or sulphate of ammonia (1 ounce to 2 gallons water). As with all liquid fertilizers, when this is done the ground must be thoroughly wet. If it has not rained recently, the soil must be given a heavy soaking. Feeding with nitrogen must not, however, be continued too long, because otherwise, soft, sappy growth, susceptible to damping off will be produced. Later in the season, while a moderate supply of nitrogen must be maintained, supplies of phosphates and potassium, to encourage root growth, ripen the wood and intensify the colour of the blooms, become of paramount importance. This is best done by feeding with one of the proprietary liquid chrysanthemum fertilizers available on the market, or by using John Innes 'L' Feed (1 ounce to 1 gallon of water). It is readily soluble, producing a clean solution without sediment. When the buds are forming and developing, a feed with a liquid manure with a high potassium content is of distinct advantage.

Mulching

Chrysanthemums appreciate plenty of moisture at their roots, therefore mulching during the warmer months with organic matter, such as composted straw, well-rotted cow or horse manure or spent hops is beneficial.

Stopping and disbudding

This subject has already been dealt with in a general way in the preceding pages. It now remains to see how the practices described are applied to early-flowering chrysanthemums. It is worthwhile repeating that the processes are nothing like so intricate as they are in the case of late-flowering varieties.

It has already been mentioned that the National Chrysanthemum Society publishes very useful stopping and timing tables. There is, however, some quite valuable information given below, which can be used by growers of early-flowering chrysanthemums. It must, of course, be borne in mind that the

Only the top 2 inches well away from the plant should be hoed.

'Trickle' irrigation waters the soil only through trickle nozzles at intervals in the hose. This system does not destroy tilth, can be regulated, and is generally accepted as the ideal method.

weather may vary the timing, in addition, that there will be some differences from variety to variety:—

(a)   Approximate time taken between stopping the main stem and the production of the first crown bud . . . seven weeks

(b)   Approximate time that passes between securing the bud of a large-flowering early and complete flowering . . . six weeks

(c)   Approximate time that passes between securing the bud of an incurving variety and complete flowering . . . eight weeks

(d)   Approximate time that passes between securing the bud of a medium early-flowering variety and complete flowering . . . four weeks

With such statistics, a chrysanthemum grower can exercise appreciable control over the time when his plants flower. It

Mulch should be placed around, but not touch, the plant. The idea is to cover the soil to conserve moisture.

could happen, for example, that blooms of a certain variety are required on a particular date for an exhibition which might be later than the normal date of flowering. Suppose the show is on the 14th of September, and it is known from experience that a chrysanthemum normally blooms in early August. It is obvious that by some method it is necessary to delay the blooming by about five weeks. It takes a large early-flowering variety about thirteen weeks from the date of stopping to the production of a fully developed bloom. Obviously, if this operation is put off, even to the extent of allowing a natural break to appear, this will cause the flowering to take place later. By simple arithmetic, however, it becomes evident that if a natural break does not appear by the first week in June, the main stem must be stopped, otherwise it will be too late. Also it should not be forgotten that the breaks highest up the stem, while being of rather shorter length, bloom first. So, when necessary, delay in blooming can be caused by cutting out the top side growths and allowing the lower ones to develop. Even after doing this, it might be found that the shoots develop too quickly and a first-crown bud, which is likely to bloom too early, is produced. The expedient then is to rub out this first-crown bud and allow the plant to run on and bloom on a side shoot from a leaf axil about two leaves lower down.

On the other hand, there are varieties of early-flowering chrysanthemums which naturally bloom late. It might, for example, be not until October. Therefore, if flowers are required in the midsummer, development of the flowers has to be accelerated. To obtain a fully developed flower by the end of July, the main stem must be stopped not later than about April 20, as a large early-flowering variety takes thirteen

Delaying flowering time. Put off stopping even to the extent of allowing the natural break to form. Flowering can be further delayed by removing higher breaks (x) and allowing selected lower ones to develop. Breaks shown in darker colour.
If selected breaks are still likely to be early, they can be retarded by removing the first crown bud and allowing a break (shown in dark colour) two leaves down to develop.

Martin Riley
Early-flowering
incurved decorative
NCS Classification 23b

Leslie Rose
Early-flowering
intermediate decorative
NCS Classification 25b

Bessie Rowe
Early-flowering
intermediate decorative
NCS Classification 25a

weeks after stopping to reach maturity. Stopping is done after the plants have been put in frames, not when they are still in the boxes or pots in which the cuttings were rooted. This means that they must be rooted early if they are to be ready by mid-summer. It is of utmost importance that there is an interval of about ten days between transplanting and stopping.

There are, of course, gardeners who are primarily interested in obtaining well-shaped and average-sized blooms as early as possible, either for cutting or garden display, not the out-size, first-quality flowers for the show bench. Such blooms can be readily obtained with present-day cultivars by removing the tip of the main stem ten to fourteen days after planting out, and by later securing the first-crown buds – picking off all side shoots below them. If extra large blooms are required, only three or four shoots are allowed to grow, each producing one bloom.

Do not secure a first-crown bud too early. The breaks should be about ½ inch long so that they can be removed without damage to the main stem. Also, allow one side

(Above) Securing bud. All unwanted buds and shoots should be removed except the one marked x. This should be kept in reserve until it is certain that the crown bud is perfect.

(Below) After securing buds, any secondary shoots appearing at the leaf axils and suckers at ground level (in darker colour) should be removed, the latter severed below the soil.

shoot to remain on the stem, when securing a bud, until it is certain that the first-crown bud is perfect. If it is damaged, it can be removed and the reserve shoot allowed to grow in its place. Similar action can be taken if the stem of a first-crown bud is unduly short.

The actual weather conditions, the latitude of the garden, its exposure and elevation all have a bearing on stopping dates. A prospective exhibitor should therefore keep records of the dates of rooting cuttings, stopping, securing the buds and flowering of the different varieties he grows. These records will prove to be invaluable in future years in planning when to carry out these operations in his particular garden.

Even after all this care has been taken, with the vagaries of the climate one cannot be absolutely sure of making the required dates. It is therefore wise to grow several plants of each variety and stop them at intervals about seven days apart, before and after the calculated date, so as to be sure of having flowers ready.

Premature buds

In some years, if the weather is hot and dry during May or June, the stems of early-flowering varieties growing out of doors become hard and brittle and the buds develop prematurely. These buds are readily distinguished by having small oval leaves growing below them. Such growths are undesirable and invariably give poor flowers. The stems should be severed at three leaves above the ground, where they should be normal in shape.

Sometimes, new growth does not develop readily from the leaf axils. Instead, strong suckers grow quite quickly. If one bud only is allowed to develop on each shoot, quite good blooms can be obtained. Some varieties produce flowers in this way which are superior to those which develop on first-crown buds.

(a) Pink Thomas Bestwick
Early-flowering reflexed decorative NCS Classification 24a
(b) Helga Taylor
Early-flowering reflexed decorative NCS Classification 24a
(c) Gay Cavalier
Early-flowering reflexed decorative NCS Classification 24b

a

b

c

A selection of early-flowering chrysanthemums

Variety	South Time of rooting	Stopping dates	North Time of rooting	Stopping dates	Scotland Time of rooting	Stopping dates
Incurved decoratives — Large-flowered NCSC 23a						
Red						
Ashover Atom	Mid Feb	10th May	Jan	7th Apl	Mid Jan	1st Apl
Yellow						
Keith Riley	Mar	N.B.	Mar	N.B.	End Feb	25th May
White						
*Ermine	Mid Feb	20th May	Jan	20th Apl	Mid Jan	5th Apl
Incurved decoratives — Medium-flowered NCSC 23b.						
Light Bronze						
(G) Topper	Mid Mar	20th May	Feb	10th May	Mid Jan	1st May
Pink						
Henley	End Feb	N.B.	Mid Feb	25th May	Feb	10th May
Yellow						
(G) Martin Riley	Mid Feb	27th May	Feb	15th May	End Jan	27th Apl
Yellow Nuggett	End Feb	N.B.	Mid Feb	N.B.	Feb	20th May
White						
Nancy Matthews	End Feb	N.B.	Feb	20th May	End Jan	10th May

Brenda Talbot
Early-flowering
intermediate decorative
NCS Classification 25b

Red

Gipsy	1st Feb	20th May	Jan		1st May	Mid Jan	20th Apl
John Shoesmith	Feb	25th May	Feb		12th May	Early Feb	1st May
Light Bronze							
Honeyglow *Peter	Mid Feb	10th May	Feb		1st May	Early Feb	15th Apl
Shoesmith	Mid Feb	20th May	Jan		7th May	Mid Jan	1st May
Pink							
Eye Catcher	Mid Feb	25th May	Jan		10th May	Mid Jan	25th Apl
Tracy Waller	Mid Feb	N.B.	Feb		25th May	End Jan	15th May
Yellow							
*Greatness	End Feb	7th Jun	Feb		25th May	Feb	15th May
White							
Rosamund Noble	Mid Feb	25th May	Feb		10th May	End Jan	1st May

Reflexed decoratives – Medium-flowered NCSC 24b.

Red

Jim Plummer	End Feb	25th May	Mid Feb	15th May	Early Feb	5th May
(G) Super Star	Mid Feb	25th May	Feb	15th May	Feb	5th May
Bronze						
(G) Capstan	Mid Feb	25th May	Feb	12th May	Feb	1st May
Kansas	End Feb	N.B.	Mid Feb	N.B.	Feb	25th May

Topper
Early-flowering
incurved decorative
NCS Classification 23b

(Left) A premature bud is recognized by mis-shaped oval upper leaves and by the dry appearance of the stem.

Plants are cut to within 3 or 4 healthy leaves from the ground.

Strong sucker growths as a result of cutting are shown in a darker colour. By restricting one bud to each of these, first class blooms can be obtained.

Orange

Variety						
Morley Jones	Mid Mar	N.B.	Mar	N.B.	Mar	25th May
Yellow						
Leslie Thomas	End Feb	5th Jun	Mid Feb	20th May	Early Feb	10th May
Purple						
Regalia	End Feb	N.B.	Feb	14th May	End Jan	1st May
(G) Starfire	Mid Mar	5th Jun	Feb	20th May	Mid Feb	10th May

Intermediate decoratives – Large-flowered NCSC 25a.

Variety						
Red						
Camp Fire	Mid Feb	7th Jun	Jan	20th May	Mid Jan	7th May
Bronze						
Doons Valley	End Feb	25th May	Feb	10th May	End Jan	1st May
Westfield Bronze	Mid Feb	25th May	Jan	20th Apl	Mid Jan	10th Apl
Pink						
John Woolman	Early Feb	25th Apl	Jan	14th Apl	Mid Jan	1st Apl
Salmon						
*Kathleen Doward	Early Feb	20th Apl	Jan	1st Apl	Mid Jan	25th Mar
Orange						
*Ethel Edmonds	Mid Feb	25th May	Feb	10th May	Mid Jan	1st May
Pale Yellow						
Alec Bedser	End Feb	5th Jun	Feb	14th May	End Jan	5th May
Purple						
Keystone	Mid Feb	20th May	Early Feb	10th May	End Jan	1st May
White						
*Evelyn Bush	Mid Feb	25th May	Feb	10th May	Mid Jan	1st May

Intermediate decoratives – Medium-flowered NCSC 25b.

Variety						
Red						
Red Setter	End Feb	N.B.	Mid Feb	N.B.	Mid Feb	20th May
Bronze						
Glen Fire	End Feb	25th Feb	Feb	14th May	End Jan	5th May
Pink						
(G) *Brenda Talbot	15th Feb	10th May	Jan	1st Apl	Mid Jan	20th Mar
Claretglow	End Feb	N.B.	Mid Feb	25th May	Early Feb	20th May
Amber Orange						
Golden Boy	End Feb	N.B.	Feb	N.B.	Feb	25th May
Yellow						
(G) *Delightful	20th Mar	N.B.	Feb	7th Jun	Mid Feb	N.B. or 20th May
(G) Fair Dinkum	Feb	15th May	Feb	5th May	Early Feb	20th Apl
Pale Yellow						
Susan Maughan	End Feb	7th May	Mid Feb	25th Apl	Feb	12th Apl
Purple						
Darkie	Early Mar	25th May	Feb	1st May	End Jan	25th Apl
White						
*Cricket	Feb	1st Jun	Feb	20th May	Early Feb	5th May

The majority of early-flowering chrysanthemums bloom on first-crown buds. N.B. = 'natural break'. Northern growers should stop N.B. varieties which have not made a natural break by 7th June. The dates given for varieties (*) apply to their colour sports. Varieties marked (G) are particularly suitable for garden display.

Polythene sheets on a timber frame provides good weather protection. In this case runner beans have been grown to provide a wind-break.

(Left) Note that the bud is showing colour, but is not sufficiently developed to have commenced opening.
(Right) Early flowering chrysanthemums after bagging. As some varieties will need bagging before others, it is advisable to date them. This will provide a rough guide for calculating the time of removal.

WEATHER PROTECTION

Early-flowering chrysanthemums are quite hardy plants. In fact, such outdoor types as sprays, pompons and Koreans are almost untouched in the worst conditions.

Exhibition chrysanthemums, however, need protection against inclement weather. Firstly, the blooms must be covered so that they remain perfect in form and colour, and so that the florets are completely undamaged. Secondly, the plants must be given protection, particularly against high winds which are so prevalent as autumn approaches.

The method for protection of the flowers depends on the number of plants grown. If large, the most effective and labour-saving way is to erect overhead covers. If small, Polythene bags or some other water-proof materials are often used, the cheapest being grease-proof paper bags. For most blooms, a 10-inch bag is sufficiently large, but occasionally a 12-inch is required. Grease-proof bags are better than polythene as they absorb surplus water and so lessen the risk of damping.

Red Setter
Early-flowering
intermediate decorative
NCS Classification 25b

Bronze Covent Garden
Early-flowering
reflexed decorative
NCS Classification 24b

The bags must be air-tight, with seams sealed with a water-proof glue, otherwise the rain will cause them to split open. It is usual to use two bags, one inside the other. They are so placed that their seams are on opposite sides.

In heavy rain, it is possible for water to enter the space between the bags and remain there. This is prevented by piercing a ring of holes, 3 inches above the opening, in the outside bag, allowing surplus water to drain away.

Prepare the bags beforehand by puncturing the outer bag and inserting the airtight one inside. Cover each bud when it is showing slight colour. Before doing this, however, spray or dust thoroughly with an insecticide containing B.H.C, DDT or derris to kill off aphids. A few experts temporarily cover each bud with a small 5-inch sweet bag immediately after spraying, inspecting it a fortnight or so later to be sure that the insecticide has been effective. The buds should not be bagged while wet or with weak necks. If they are wet or weak leave them for a couple of days, after which they will stiffen and be strong enough to bear the weight of the bags. Generally speaking, if the buds show colour, their necks are strong enough. Before putting the bags into position, label and date them. To soften the paper the lower $\frac{1}{2}$ inch at the mouth of each bag is dipped into water. To protect the florets ultimately from gales, flatten the top corners and inflate the bags. Place the bags over a bud, with the bottom covering the stem by about 2 inches. Shape the lower part around the stem, and tie with two-ply fillis or a paper-covered wire. Other ties can be made to just below the bud. When finally tied, it is supported with the left hand, and with the right gently pressed down to take up the shape into which it is desired the bloom should develop. When the maturity date is reached, remove the bags piece by piece after cutting with a razor blade.

An alternative method of protecting is to erect permanent supports, which carry polythene covers or frame lights above the plants. While this method gives good protection against rain, it has the disadvantage of encouraging damping of the blooms when the weather is warm and humid. Since the development of young buds depends upon their having the maximum of light and early-morning dew, it is important that the frame lights are not put into position too early.

CHRYSANTHEMUMS FOR GARDEN DISPLAY

Undoubtedly, the majority of the early-flowering varieties are grown for display in the garden. Apart from staking, they are no more difficult to cultivate than other plants. It is usual to plant them 18 inches apart, about the middle of May. There are no very strict rules about stopping them. For most practical purposes, it is sufficient to pinch out the tip of the main stem ten to fourteen days after they have been transferred to the open. Gardeners who require compact bushes usually stop their plants for a second time by removing the tips of the first breaks.

Outdoor pompons

Pompons are lovely chrysanthemums, invaluable for borders, pots and cutting. If not disbudded, they are unparalleled in their profusion of flowers. Some of the newer varieties will produce as many as 200 to each plant. Their colour range is wonderful, embracing red, orange, golden-yellow, chestnut-brown, rose-pink, strawberry and a host of others. Perhaps their greatest virtue is compactness. Heights generally vary from 9 inches to 2 feet, while a few reach 3 feet. Many of the blooms are ball-shaped, with petals tightly bound and hard in texture.

A selection of pompons for garden display

Red	Bronze Fairie	**Pink**	Joy
Imp	Bronze Gremlin	Gremlin	**Orange**
Bob	Picolino	**Yellow**	Lustre
Bronze	**Purple**	Denise	**White**
Beeswing	Masquerade	Jante Wells	Cameo

Some are as little as $\frac{1}{2}$ inch in diameter, while others approach the size of a tennis ball.

Their propagation is much the same as that of earlies. Cuttings are rooted at a minimum temperature of 48°F to 50°F. If a heated greenhouse is available, these can be taken early in the year, otherwise, it is better to delay until the middle of March, or even a little later if it is very cold. The cuttings are prepared in the same manner as previously described and planted 2 inches apart in a box or round the edge of a pot, using John Innes Potting Compost No. 1 as the growing medium. On potting, the cuttings should be watered and maintained at a temperature of 50°F, shading them with newspaper if the sunshine is strong. They are transplanted to their flowering quarters from the end of April onwards, depending

87

upon the weather. They can also be propagated by root division in autumn or early spring, or by rooted off-sets in the spring. Stopping and, in most cases, staking are unnecessary. To maintain continuous blooming, however, dead-heading is important.

Outdoor spray varieties

For quite a long time there have been available a number of greenhouse chrysanthemums which are known as spray varieties. In more recent times, early-flowering garden spray cultivars have been introduced and become highly sought-after, producing an abundance of flowers, both single and double, and covering an almost inexhaustible range of colour. They are indispensable for floral arrangements, so much so that they are now as popular as their indoor counterparts. They have a long flowering season, usually from mid-August well into October, and range in height from 2 to 3 feet.

From the point of view of cultivation, they are easy to grow.

Spray variety—
Golden Orfe

The majority are short and bushy and need little support. Their compactness is encouraged by breaking out the first $\frac{1}{2}$ to $\frac{3}{4}$ inch of the shoots about three weeks after the middle of May, when they were planted.

A recent introduction is the hardy spray chrysanthemums. It is claimed that they will withstand the winter. They come into bloom in spring and continue flowering until the autumn frosts. If they live up to their promise, they will certainly revolutionize chrysanthemum growing.

A selection of spray chrysanthemums for garden cultivation

Red	**Apricot Pink**	Lilian Hoek
Red Pye	Apricot Charming	**Yellow**
Troef	**Salmon**	Golden Orfe
Pink	Wally Ruff	Goude Elsje
Pink Glory	**Bronze**	Joke
Rosette Queen	Sonnegold	**White**
Daphne	**Orange**	Garden White

Spray variety–
Charming

89

Spoon chrysanthemums

These are very charming outdoor chrysanthemums. Their variously coloured petals each terminate in the shape of a spoon

A selection of spoon chrysanthemums for garden display

Red	**Yellow**	**Pale Yellow**
Charm Spoon	Shining Light	Moonlight Spoon
Pink	**White**	**Purple Gold**
Tickled Pink	White Spoon	Garnet Spoon
Orange		
Gretel		

Korean chrysanthemums

Korean chrysanthemums were first introduced into Great Britain in 1937. Since then they have rapidly risen in popularity. This is largely because they are hardy and provide colour after frost has spoiled the early-flowering chrysanthemums.

They are well-shaped, bushy plants varying in height from 1 foot to as high as $3\frac{1}{2}$ feet. The more compact varieties form cushions of the bright single or double flowers.

They are very easy to grow, needing little attention. Tall varieties need support against autumn winds. Chrysanthemums planted in late April or early May will produce masses of

Koreans—Otley Beauty

Koreans—
Gold Lust

A selection of Korean chrysanthemums for garden display

Bronze	Red	Yellow
Betty	Herb Miles	Gert Raynor
Orange	Rip Joice	Yellow Tench
Blondie	Otley Beauty	Glint
Sunrise	Stan Joice	Gold Lust
Lavender	**Pink**	Noon
Ivy Joice	Coquette	
Purple	Melody	
Twinkle	Rita Tench	
Cream	Startler	
Ada Miles		

blooms by August. To help them make a good start, watering is important for a time after planting. Dig and manure the soil the previous winter. Set the plants 18 to 24 inches apart.

They can be propagated from cuttings, or in the spring by division of established clumps. They are also grown from seeds set in good compost in February and March and kept at a temperature between 50°F and 55°F. Seedlings can be planted at the end of April or early May.

Korean chrysanthemums give a massed colour display well into the autumn. Their uses in the garden are numerous. They prolong the colour in herbaceous borders until late autumn, and are invaluable for the front of a shrub border, imparting brightness long after summer colour has passed.

Some gardeners like to use them in their formal beds in which a succession of plants such as wallflowers, forget-me-nots, sweet williams, nemesia and *Phlox drummondii* is planted, because they provide a fresh green foil to the other occupants. Later they continue the colour display well into autumn in their own right.

Chrysanthemum rubellum

Rubellums are vivid, very attractive chrysanthemums with gay colours enhanced by attractive foliage. The flowers are large, on branched sprays, long-lasting and excellent for cutting. They can be grown alone or in a mixed border.

They grow in most soils that retain moisture yet are well drained and like all chrysanthemums they do not like water-logged ground. They are absolutely hardy, blooming from early August until November.

Propagation is by root division, seed or cuttings, and cultivation is similar to that for early-flowering chrysanthemums, but they need no staking or disbudding. The planting season is during the whole of April and early May. Setting them in a sunny position will ensure a long-lasting display. They look best if planted in groups of three or more, because their lovely foliage shows up their gay colours better than if individual plants are dotted about the beds.

A selection of *Chrysanthemum rubellum* for garden display

Duchess of Edinburgh	Glowing red
Jessie Cooper	Copper red
Red Ensign	Deep red
Anna Hay	Pastel shade of shell pink
Ann, Lady Brockett	Pinky apricot
Clara Curtis	Pink
Prince Charles	Pink
Princess Margaret	Pink
Vagabond	Pink
Mary Stoker	Soft canary-yellow
Paul Boissier	Orange-bronze

Chrysanthemum rubellum grows into neat, compact bushes, about 2 feet in height, with rather stiff, strong stems. In an exposed garden they may be supported with twiggy sticks placed around the plants to keep them upright.

Charm chrysanthemums for garden display

Charm chrysanthemums are particularly lovely plants, first introduced into this country about twenty years ago. These early introductions were for growing in greenhouses. At that

time they were received with great enthusiasm. Today, varieties are available which will thrive out of doors, and are equally as beautiful as the greenhouse cultivars. As the illustration shows, they are reminiscent of Japanese azaleas and can be effectively planted in similar positions in the border.

They form small, low-growing, spreading bushes 2 to 3 feet in diameter, and reaching a height of 18 inches. When fully developed, they are covered with small blooms, about the size of Michaelmas daises. They have an exceptional range of the most delightful colours, including white and many shades of red, pink, yellow and bronze. It is not yet possible to buy named varieties.

This brilliant show of colour is maintained continuously from mid-August to mid-October. The flowers have a delicate, sweet scent. They should be planted out in May, wherever massed colour is needed. They can be effectively used at the

Charm chrysanthemums, showing the great number of flowers produced on one plant. They are particularly well suited for borders and have a delightful range of colour.

edges of borders, and where space permits, growers are well advised to plant these lovely chrysanthemums. Cuttings require very little attention beyond stopping in late May or early June after they are well established.

Chrysanthemum maximum—
Cobham Gold

Chrysanthemum maximum

Many nurserymen list these plants in catalogues of herbaceous plants. This often puzzles gardeners, because it is unusual to find chrysanthemums included among such subjects.

Except under extremely wet and cold conditions, the plants are very hardy. They like very rich, well-drained soil, but it matters little whether it is clay or light, sandy loam, providing it has good drainage and contains the nutriments that they need. It is impossible to overfeed them. They are readily propagated by taking rooted shoots during the late summer. These shoots should be planted 12 to 18 inches apart. Providing they are well looked after and given the conditions they like, they suffer little from disease. All varieties of *Chrysanthemum maximum* must be divided every year. They range from $1\frac{1}{2}$ to 4 feet in height.

A selection of *Chrysanthemum maximum* for garden display

Ben Lomond	Extra large fringed white blooms.
Cobham Gold	Rich, butter-coloured, darkening towards the centre.
Droitwich Beauty	White, somewhat shaggy flowers. Has tall stiff stalks and foliage.
Esther Read	Large double white flowers with bright green foliage.
Everest	Large, single, pure white, with rigid stems.
Joan Reeves	Extra large flowers, with yellow, cushion-like centres and creamy white petals.
John Murray	Pure white, double flowers, up to 5 inches in diameter, on long stems.
Moonlight	Large, double white flushed with yellow, growing on long stems.
Phyllis Smith	Large, white, fringed blooms on rigid stems.
Snowball	A rather unusual dwarf cultivar, with ball-like flowers. Very useful in the garden and for cutting.
Thomas Killan	Large, white, anemone-centred flowers, often as much as $5\frac{1}{2}$ inches in diameter, borne on strong, upright stems.
Wirral Pride	An anemone-centred chrysanthemum with very large, pure white blooms. Forms well-branched sprays.
Wirral Supreme	Double, white flowers, growing on bushy plants, up to $3\frac{1}{2}$ feet high.

This is the best method of removing a plant from a 3″ pot. The plant illustrated has a good root system.

LATE-FLOWERING CHRYSANTHEMUMS

Late-flowering chrysanthemums live for most of the summer in pots in the open. As they bloom after the bad weather has set in, they are brought into a greenhouse in September. Late-flowering cultivars are grown in pots for exhibition, cutting or decorative purposes. To obtain the best results, it is important for the grower to acquire a first-class knowledge of his subjects so that he can obtain the right sort of blooms at the correct time. He must know their many characteristics.

These characteristics not only vary with the different types, but also from variety to variety. Even buds on plants of the same varieties differ at the various stages of their growth. Sometimes, first-crown buds have a large number of tightly packed florets, malforming the blooms. These cultivars are best run on to second-crown buds.

Perfect flowers are impossible to produce without good cultivation. No subsequent devices or gimmicks or tricks of the trade, or whatever else they may be called, can possibly produce them unless they are efficiently raised. The methods used for early and late-flowering chrysanthemums are identical until the cuttings are rooted. After this, the procedures followed for each are different. While early-flowering ones are planted in the open ground, the late-flowering varieties usually spend the whole of their lives in pots.

Indoor varieties need to build up a healthy root system. This is achieved by transplanting the plants at each stage into larger pots. This process is vital to their well-being.

Potting procedure

When the cuttings have been planted for some weeks, and are growing healthily, they are re-potted into 3-inch diameter pots. In former times, clay pots were used, but nowadays plastic and 'whale-hide' pots are largely utilized, especially by commercial growers. Pots composed of peat are especially suitable for this first planting, as they encourage young plants to make rapid growth. The potting medium at this stage is John Innes Potting Compost No. 2, lightly pressed round the roots.

Having removed the plant it should be placed in a larger (5'' to 6'') pot

Avoid pressure which might damage them. Fill the pots to about 1 inch from the rim, so allowing for watering. Water should be used sparingly. For about ten days, the young plants might flag, but as soon as they are robust again they should be placed in a cool frame. They need plenty of air, but dislike draughts. At this stage, the young shoots are particularly attractive to insects, and should be sprayed at least once a fortnight with an insecticide. Malathion, liquid derris or Lindane are suitable for this purpose. When the roots fully fill the pots, which is clearly shown by their protruding through the drain holes, transfer the plants to 5 or 6-inch pots, using John Innes Compost No. 3. The timing of transplanting is very important because, if chrysanthemums become pot-bound, their growth is seriously hindered.

This second potting is usually necessary some six or seven weeks after the rooted cuttings have been first planted. Traditionally, the soil is consolidated firmly around the roots at this stage, but

The pots are prevented from blowing over by tying each stake to a horizontal wire fixed to a post at each end of the row.

more recent thinking advocates filling the pots and only tapping the soil down.

About the middle of May, the chrysanthemums are transplanted into 8, 9 or 10-inch pots, according to their vigour. They can be planted in John Innes Potting Compost No. 4.

Traditionally, the soil is well firmed, using a rammer, but modern practice dictates that it is only necessary to tap the soil down around the roots. To allow for watering, a 2-inch space should be left at the top of the pot. At the same time as planting, a stake of appropriate length should be inserted alongside the main stem and the plant securely, but not tightly, tied.

After this potting, the chrysanthemums are put out in the open for the summer, well spaced in rows, standing on a hard surface, such as boards, well-consolidated ashes or gravel, so as to deter the roots from entering the ground. A walking space should be left between the rows to give easy access for maintenance. To prevent the chrysanthemums blowing over in high winds, the stakes should be tied to horizontal wires, running along the rows, fastened to posts at either end.

With clay pots one method of testing if the plant needs water is to gently tap the pot. If it 'rings' the plant needs water, otherwise it will give a dull thud.

Prior to housing, the lower
leaves should be removed. After
cleaning the pot, the plant
should be sprayed with fungicide.

Large exhibition varieties (formerly called Japanese or incurving Japanese)

Chrysanthemums have for a long time been appreciated for their value in decorating the home and garden, and the proportion of members of the National Chrysanthemum Society who raise them purely for exhibition purposes is almost certainly small. However, quite a number of people who start by raising chrysanthemums for decorative purposes go on to enter the competitive world of the show and to grow large exhibition cultivars.

Cuttings are taken in December and January and if maintained at a temperature of around 50°F should be ready for their first potting in early February. Further potting is carried out as described on pages 99–101.

The blooms of large exhibition cultivars, which are mainly raised for exhibition purposes, are nearly always grown on first-crown buds. It is a well established fact that best flowers are produced in November, when late-flowering chrysanthemum shows are held, from buds secured between 7th and 20th of August. Buds appearing earlier do not give good blooms, while those ready for securing in early September seldom develop in time and, when they do, give inferior flowers. Thus, to get the best results, it is necessary to work to a schedule by which the buds are ready to be secured between the dates mentioned. It is, at the same time, important to restrict the number of blooms on each plant to two.

A number of large exhibition cultivars are natural break varieties – they send out lateral shoots without being stopped. If cuttings are taken in January, this usually occurs during May, when all the breaks are removed except two, which develop first-crown buds about the middle of August, when they are secured. The stopping and timing of large exhibition chrysanthemums is more intricate than that of early-flowering varieties. Beginners are therefore advised to concentrate initially on natural-break cultivars. If any of these, however, do not make a natural break by the last week of May, they must be stopped by removing the tip of the main stem.

Apart from natural-break varieties, there are a large number of cultivars which need to be stopped. Timing particulars for these are given in the National Chrysanthemum Society's

A selection of large exhibition chrysanthemums NCSC section 1

Variety	South Time of rooting	Stopping dates	North Time of rooting	Stopping dates	Scotland Time of rooting	Stopping dates
Red						
James Bryant Lilian	End Nov	6th Mar	Nov	1st Mar	Mid Nov	Mid Feb
Smallwood	Mid Jan	N.B.	Dec	20th May	Mid Dec	10th May
Pink						
J. S. Dakers	Early Jan	N.B.	Dec	15th May	Mid Dec	7th May
Lilac Prince	Early Jan	20th May	Dec	25th Apl	Mid Dec	15th Apl
Monica Bennett	Jan	20th Apl	Dec	10th Apl	Dec	1st Apl
Woking Rose Woolman's	Early Jan	25th May	Dec	10th May	Mid Dec	1st May
Victor	Early Jan	N.B.	Dec	15th May	Mid Dec	5th May
Salmon Pink						
Gigantic	End Dec	25th May	Dec	10th May	Dec	1st May
Orange						
Arthur Blythe Saint	End Dec	20th May	Dec	10th May	Dec	1st May
Edmundsbury	Mid Jan	N.B.	Dec	25th May	Mid Dec	10th May
Yellow						
Albert Shoesmith	End Dec	N.B.	Dec	1st May	Mid Dec	25th Apl
*Harold Habgood	Early Jan	25th May	Dec	10th May	Mid Dec	5th May
Mark Woolman	End Dec	15th Apl	Dec	10th Apl	Mid Dec	5th Apl
Patricia Barnett	Early Jan	1st Jun	Dec	20th May	Mid Dec	10th May
Purple						
Peter May	Early Jan	14th May	Dec	7th May	End Dec	12th Apl
White						
*Jessie Habgood	End Dec	10th May	Dec	1st May	Mid Dec	20th Apl
*Duke of Kent	End Dec	20th May	Dec	10th May	Mid Dec	7th Apl

Notes

N.B. = 'natural break'. Southern and northern growers should stop N.B. varieties which have not made a natural break by the last week of May.

The dates given for varieties marked (*) apply to their colour sports.

All large exhibition chrysanthemums should be flowered on first-crown buds.

Late-flowering
large exhibition varieties
NCS Classification 1

(Top) Paul Habgood
(Bottom) Duke of Kent

publication *Chrysanthemum Stopping and Timing*.

Securing the buds consists of removing all the breaks growing on the stems below the first-crown buds when about $\frac{3}{4}$ inch long. Sometimes a bud is developing too quickly to meet the date when the bloom is required. Such growths can be retarded by delaying the securing of the buds until the side shoots are about 2 inches long. Whenever the lateral shoots are removed, great care must be taken not to tear the skin of the stem. In addition, since bud development in large exhibition varieties naturally takes place during the dark hours, it can be retarded by exposing the plant to artificial light for part of the night, or hastened by keeping it in a dark place, in a cellar or under a black polythene cover for some time during daylight hours.

Large exhibition chrysanthemums do not bloom until November, or even later, when the autumn frost could damage

Peter May Late-flowering large exhibition
NCS Classification 1

Arthur Blythe Late-flowering large exhibition
NCS Classification 1

them if left out of doors. Consequently, in late September they must be brought into a greenhouse, which has been cleaned and fumigated. The plants themselves should be sprayed with an insecticide and all the dead leaves low down on the plant should be removed.

The plants at this stage are subject to 'damping', which is caused by excessively warm and humid conditions. The disease is avoided by applying ventilation without excessive heat. Heat provided by an oil-burning lamp or a length of electrical tubular heating, with carefully controlled ventilation, is a simple way of minimizing the risk of infection, but the use of an elaborate fan-type heater can go quite a long way towards solving the problem.

The feeding of chrysanthemums has already been discussed. It is, however, vitally important to remember that a plant must never at any time be allowed to show signs of starvation.

Medium exhibition

This is a classification that has more recently been revised by the National Chrysanthemum Society. Some of the smaller large exhibition cultivars have been transferred into this section. It is currently a comparatively small category but it does contain some varieties which are particularly good as cut flowers.

Cuttings are taken in December and January, after which they are treated in the same manner as large exhibition types.

Medium exhibition cultivars are flowered on first-crown buds. It is usual to stop most varieties between the middle of April and mid-May, when the number of side shoots should be reduced to three to six shoots, according to the size and quality of blooms desired. Natural-break varieties must be stopped if the breaks do not appear by May 20. When the first-crown buds have developed, they are secured so that they bloom in October or early November.

A selection of medium-flowering chrysanthemums, according to the NCS classification section 2 is *red*, Birmingham, Cossack; *pink*, Rita Shirley; *yellow*, Connie Mayhew, Jim Stacey, Monica Winterton and Winn Quinn.

Exhibition incurved cultivars

Cuttings are rooted in January. If the weather is reasonably warm they will normally break naturally about the middle of June. When this occurs, all but three of the side shoots are removed. When the first-crown buds appear, usually early in September, they are secured. By so doing, flowers can be expected to be fully developed by early November. In cooler districts it is necessary to stop in mid-May to achieve flowering by this date.

They can also be flowered on second-crown buds. In this method, two stopping dates, which are suitable for most exhibition incurved varieties are April 15 and June 15. On the first date, the tip of the main stem is removed and all the lateral shoots except three.

In June, each main stem is stopped again by breaking out the tip. The next procedure depends on whether the blooms are required for exhibition or as cut flowers. In the former case, only one side shoot is allowed to remain on each stem. If they are required for cutting, up to three breaks can be left on each stem to obtain nine good blooms.

Cossack Late-flowering medium exhibition NCS Classification 2

A selection of exhibition incurved chrysanthemums

NCS Classification Section 3a

Light Bronze
Lilian Shoesmith
Souvenir
Welcome News
Pink
Audrey Shoesmith
Mavis Shoesmith
Magna Carta
Shirley Model

Yellow
Dexta
John Rowe
Yellow Marvel
White
Shirley Crystal
Woolman's Perfecta

NCS Classification Section 3b

Bronze
Waterloo
Light Bronze
Buff Maylen
Frances Jefferson
Herbert Cuerden
Minstrel Boy
Walter Warner
Pink
Mary Rowe
Pale Pink
Pink Cloud

Yellow
Blazing Gold
Vera Woolman
Yellow Bickleigh
Yellow Brocade
Yellow Ron Shoesmith
White
Donna
Maylen
Ron Shoesmith
Silver Knight

(Opposite page) Ron Shoesmith
Late-flowering
exhibition incurved
NCS Classification 3b

(This page, top) Frances Jefferson
Late-flowering
exhibition incurved
NCS Classification 3b
(Below) Maria Shoesmith
Late-flowering
exhibition incurved
NCS Classification 3a

Decorative (reflexed and intermediate)

The reflexed decoratives have florets gracefully reflexing, while in the intermediate decorative class there are varieties that have incurved florets and others that are semi-reflexing and bicoloured. Cuttings of decoratives are taken later than those of the late-flowering chrysanthemums already discussed, usually between mid-January and mid-February. There are, however, a few varieties which flower too early, particularly in the South, for the November shows. The rooting of cuttings of such varieties is therefore deferred to the end of March.

Cuttings taken in January or February are ready for their first potting into 3-inch pots in early March. At the next stage, about early April, they are transplanted to $4\frac{1}{2}$-inch pots. Five weeks later, they are potted into 8, 9 or 10-inch pots, according to their vigour. When blooms are required for cut flowers it is possible to bed out the rooted cuttings in frames, and then to transplant them into their final pots, once they have built up a large enough root-system. This saves considerable labour.

Most decorative varieties give best blooms on first-crown buds, but there are a few intermediates which produce better results if allowed to run on to second-crown buds.

Glen shades
Late-flowering
intermediate decorative
NCS Classification 5b

Fair Lady
Late-flowering
intermediate decorative
NCS Classification 5a

When flowering these chrysanthemums on first-crown buds, the plants are stopped once by removing the tip of the main stem. A number of decorative chrysanthemums are natural-break varieties, particularly when grown in the South. It is usual to allow up to nine breaks to develop, according to the purpose for which the flowers are required. Ten days should elapse after re-potting before stopping is carried out.

For second-crown buds, the first stopping is carried out when the plants are still in $4\frac{1}{2}$ inch pots, as soon as the breaks commence to develop. Three side shoots, which should all be of uniform size, are allowed to grow.

After the chrysanthemums have been transferred to their final pots each side shoot is stopped. This normally must not be done later than mid-June. The number of lateral shoots left on each of these stems at this stage depends upon whether the blooms are intended for cutting or exhibition. For cutting, three shoots on each stem are generally allowed to develop, giving nine blooms, whereas for the latter purpose, the development of two usually gives six very satisfactory blooms.

Desert Song
Late-flowering single
NCS Classification 7a

Singles

For both exhibition and cutting, this is a very attractive class of chrysanthemum. A single cultivar is defined as one in which each bloom has no more than five rows of ray florets. The best blooms are obtained when they are flowered on second-crown buds. Those on first-crown buds are often semi-double.

The rooted cuttings which, like the decoratives, are taken between mid-January and mid-February, are first potted in 3-inch pots in early March. When fully developed, the plants are transplanted to $4\frac{1}{2}$ or 5-inch pots, about a month later. The final potting usually takes place about the end of May, when unlike the decorative varieties, single chrysanthemums are potted in $8\frac{1}{2}$-inch pots.

The first stopping is invariably done when the plants are still in $4\frac{1}{2}$ or 5-inch pots. It is usual to allow only two side shoots to continue to develop. The timing of the second stop varies according to whether the cultivars are large or medium flowered. For large varieties, the general recommendation is the second week in June – about two weeks after they have been transferred to their final pots. The mediums are stopped for the second time about one week later. Each of the two laterals, which have developed after the first stopping, have their tips removed and breaks on each are removed to leave only three. Thus, six blooms are produced on each plant. The second-crown buds, which ultimately develop, are secured during the first two weeks in September.

A selection of single varieties

Large-flowered
Red
Autumn Shirley
Bronze
Desert Song
Woolman's Glory
Pink
Preference
Yellow
Peggy Stevens
Shirley Sunshine

Medium-flowered
Red
Chesswood Beauty
Pink
Wychwood
Orange
Nautilus
Yellow
Golden Seal
Nancy Sherwood

Cheerful
Late-flowering single
NCS Classification 7b

Crimson Betty Rose
Late-flowering
anemone
NCS Classification 6a

Bronze Fairy
Early-flowering
pompon
NCS Classification 28a

Anemones

Although these cultivars are not popular for showing, they have lovely flowers and are particularly beautiful when flowered as sprays. Their cultivation, if grown as single specimens, is similar to that for singles.

A selection of anemones

Red
Raymond Mounsey
Crimson Betty Rose
Bronze
Red Rolinda
Light Bronze
Amber Long Island Beauty
Rolinda
Nebula
Mauve-Pink
Elspeth
Lilac Pink
Orchid Beauty

Yellow
Yellow Long Island Rose
Primrose Long Island Beauty
Sulphur Long Island Beauty
Yellow Rolinda
White
Grace Land
Long Island Beauty
Pink
Betty Rose
Denebola

Pompons

These beautiful indoor chrysanthemums are frequently allowed to bloom in sprays. At their best, each plant is laden with small compact flowers. Their cultivation is almost identical with that of the decoratives. They are stopped twice, but no laterals are removed. The first time is when they are in $4\frac{1}{2}$-inch pots, and the second takes places not later than about the end of the second week in June. Every bud is allowed to flower.

A selection of pompon varieties

Bronze
November Midget
November Bronze
Yellow
Baby
Fortyniner
Golden Climax
Golden New York
Tansy

Pale Pink
Popcorn
Bristolite
Pink
Elmerinda
Dresden China
Mdlle Elise Dordon
Purple
Atco

Specimen plants

These plants, grown in pots, no longer feature greatly in shows, conservatories and drawing rooms as they did at the turn of the century. At that time the classes for single specimens were keenly contested. However, there is still a place for such plants on the show bench. To ensure success, the cultivation of these plants calls for considerable skill and many tedious hours staking, feeding and training.

The most intriguing aspect of this form of chrysanthemum growing is the phenomenal number of blooms that each well-cultivated plant can be made to produce. Experts recommend that the number of blooms on various members of the 'Curry family' (Golden Curry and Annie Curry), which are eminently suitable for this purpose, should not be allowed to exceed 130. There are cultivars which grow as many as 300, but this can only be done at the expense of the quality of the flowers. Gardeners interested in cultivating this type of chrysanthemum are advised to consult *The Chrysanthemum Manual* of the National Chrysanthemum Society.

Framework for specimen plant.
Wire loops are secured to canes.

Golden Curry. Specimen plants can have upwards of 120 blooms and be 3 to 5 feet in diameter. Late-flowering large exhibition NCS Classification 1a

Dwarf pot plants

Dwarf pot plants, some of which are naturally dwarf, can be cultivated by anybody who has a greenhouse.

A selection of naturally dwarf chrysanthemums

Red
Ami Perroid
Spanish Lady
Yellow
Incurving Yellow Morin

Purple
Cochineal
Jean Cot Improved
White
Blanche Poitevene
Marie Morin

In addition, there are many chrysanthemums grown nowadays, especially by commercial growers, that are artificially dwarfed. In more recent years, scientists have developed a number of chemicals which have the effect of stunting

Yellow Hammer Charm variety

growth. The three most commonly used are Cycocel or C.C.C., B Nine or B_{995} and Phosfon. Phosfon is added to the potting compost.

Indoor charm chrysanthemums

Charm chrysanthemums are very lovely pot plants which give masses of small, sweet smelling and exquisitely coloured blooms for as long as eight weeks from October onwards. They are invaluable for decorative purposes and give brightness as the more gloomy days of winter approach. They are relatively easy to raise, either from seed sown in early February, or from cuttings started in March and April. Their cultivation is very similar to that of the late-flowering decoratives, except that they are only stopped once, when they are a few inches high. Staking is unnecessary.

It is not uncommon for plants to grow to 3 feet in diameter and to 18 to 24 inches high. Up to 1,000 blooms at a time are by no means unattainable. There are many colours – red, crimson, rose-pink, yellow, blush white and white.

Cascade chrysanthemums

These have colourful blooms very much like charm chrysan-themums. They produce masses of flowers from the end of October to December, giving a wonderful display in the green house. They are grown in pots, and the best effect is obtained if they are placed on a high shelf, so that their long pendulous stems flow downwards like a cascade. They can also be trained into bush form.

Their cultivation is similar to that of the large exhibition and decorative cultivars. However, considerable skill is required when stalking and tying, but the enthusiastic amateur should not be put off as the result of such labour is well worth the effort involved.

Deep Crimson Cascade variety

CHRYSANTHEMUM DISEASES

Although a number of proprietary brands of fungicides and insecticides are recommended in the next two sections, users are advised to exercise extreme caution in their use, especially if a root crop is grown nearby, because of their toxicity.

Aspermy

The appearance of flowers affected by this virus varies from variety to variety (see page 126). Some show severe twisting of the ray florets, while in others these become spiky and tubular. Sometimes they are ragged and the ray florets, especially red, bronze and pink, have blemishes of lighter colour over them ('breaking of the colour') – a sure sign of the disease.

Affected plants should be burnt immediately, even if only a few blooms are slightly damaged. Infected plants must not be used for propagation. The virus is carried by aphids which can be controlled by using an insecticide, see page 130.

Botrytis (Damping of blooms)

This is caused by the fungus *Botrytis cineria,* attacking both indoor and outdoor varieties. It is encouraged by warm humid conditions, particularly when the temperature is about 75°F. Commercial growers can do very little to prevent the disease attacking their outdoor plants, but amateurs, with a small number, can cover them with grease-proof bags in the same way as they protect their blooms against bad weather.

In the greenhouse, the risk of infection can be minimized by controlling the heat and ventilation, so that warm, humid conditions are avoided, especially at night. Orthocide (Captan) dust has proved effective when applied through a puffer, just as the buds are beginning to burst.

Excessive feeding of nitrogen should be avoided because there is evidence that chrysanthemums so treated are more susceptible to botrytis.

Chrysanthemum rust

This disease, which is a danger to outdoor plants, particularly those grown commercially, is caused by the fungus *Puccinia chrysanthemi*, which is specific to chrysanthemums. The spores are dispersed either by wind or splashed water.

At the onset of the disease, pale coloured freckles appear on the upper leaf surfaces. In about two days, under each fleck, dark brown powdery spore pustules form on the undersides of the leaves. As the disease spreads, the leaves dry and die. By this time they have assumed a characteristic dirty appearance.

The spores will continue to live on the leaves after the chrysanthemums have died. It is important therefore to cut all old stems down to the ground and burn them. On no account propagate from affected plants.

Control the disease by spraying a fungicide on to the leaves, so that spores coming in contact with them cannot germinate. This is done by spraying the plants with a liquid spray of wettable sulphur, or the fungicide 'Thiram'.

Crown and leafy gall

This disease is caused by a bacterium, *Corynebacterium fascians*. It produces short, thick, twisted and distorted buds and shoots at the base of the stems. There is no known cure, so affected plants must be burnt.

(*Above*)
Chrysanthemum rust
(*Below*) A selection of fumigation products

KARATHANE CANISTER

BHC SMOKE

DDT PELLETS

It is a very infectious disease, and articles coming in contact with it, including tools and hands, must be sterilized. New chrysanthemum stock should not be planted in the same ground for at least two years.

Powdery mildew

This disease is caused by the fungus *Erysiphe cichoracearum*, producing a powdery white growth particularly on the undersides of the leaves. The chrysanthemums, which might be either outdoor or greenhouse types, when infected, lose their vigour and the leaves turn brown and fall off.

There is a greater risk of attack if the plants are allowed to dry out. It is important therefore to keep the soil moist. They should also be provided with plenty of air.

To control the disease a protective layer of fungicide should

Powdery Mildew

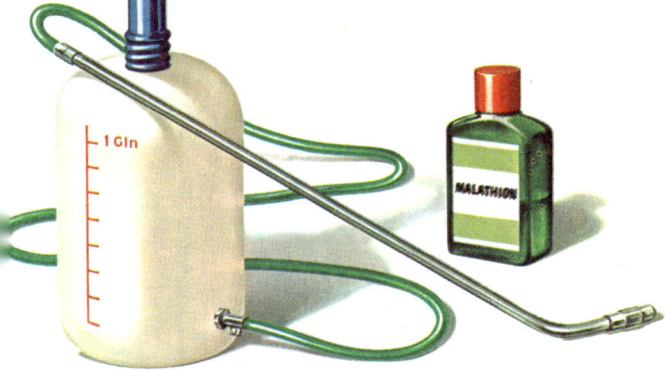

A spray of the type illustrated is both efficient and inexpensive. A webbing harness can easily be fitted to leave both hands free.

be maintained on the surface of the leaves, particularly the undersides. This can be effectively done by treating them with Karathane, either as a spray or, if in the greenhouse, in the form of a smoke.

Septoria leaf spot

This fungus disease is serious. It attacks garden chrysanthemums, but can also be serious in greenhouses, particularly when the ventilation is bad. It is caused by two fungi belonging to the same family, *Septoria chrysanthemella* and *Septoria obesa*. They invade the plant by entering the undersides of the leaves. Their spores are spread principally by splashed water. Consequently it is found that the onslaught of the disease is less severe during a dry season.

The disease first reveals itself by the presence of round spots up to $\frac{1}{2}$ inch in diameter on the lower leaves. Initially they are yellow-green, turning brown and ultimately deep brown or black. As the disease develops, the spots become larger and join up, at which stage the leaves die and hang lifeless from the stem. In this condition, the plants display the appearance of having been attacked by eelworm. It is only possible to

Plant with aspermy virus

Plant with spotted wilt

Healthy plant—Sussex Yellow

distinguish between the damage caused by nematodes and that of the septoria fungi by microscopic examination.

The disease can be controlled by strict attention to hygiene and by the use of fungicides. As the spores winter on the infected foliage, it is imperative to gather and burn all damaged leaves in autumn. Cuttings and root divisions must not be taken from infected plants.

Copper-based fungicides, such as bordeaux mixture, give excellent protection. Spray the lower sides of leaves, as it is there that spores enter the plants, as soon as signs appear.

Spotted wilt

Fortunately, this virus disease does not appear frequently in Great Britain. The first symptom is the appearance of one or two yellow rings on some of the leaves. Later, light green spots develop on the younger leaves, while brown blemishes appear on the older ones. Soon, the leaves are distorted and begin to

Plant with septoria leaf spot

curl downwards. The plants become generally unhealthy and growth is retarded. In this case, the disease is conveyed from one plant to another by thrips, which must be relentlessly attacked. There is no known cure, so all plants infected with spotted wilt must be destroyed without delay.

Verticillium wilt

This is a very serious disease of chrysanthemums grown commercially for cutting. It is also common in private gardens. The disease manifests itself by the paling of the lower leaves accompanied by wilting of their edges. As the attack gets a hold, the whole leaf wilts and dies. At first the lower leaves are attacked, but gradually it works its way up the stem. There are, however, some cultivars in which the onslaught is confined to the lower portion of the plant. Again, there are others where the disease shows itself by the production of red foliage as colder conditions occur in the autumn. One of the most striking features of the disease is in the initial stage when the appearance of the symptoms is one-sided – sometimes only part of the plant is affected, even one side of a stem. Later, however, the whole chrysanthemum plant falls victim to the disease. Another peculiarity is that cuttings and young plants, even if infected, show no symptoms. It is only after the buds set that the disease appears.

The fungus verticillium is responsible for the damage. Unfortunately, it is nearly always present in the soil. There is little that can be done to control the fungus, except to destroy affected plants. If they are used for cuttings, disease-ridden plants will be produced. When an attack of verticillium wilt is confirmed, it is wise to obtain a fresh stock of chrysanthemums from a reputable nurseryman. Do not, however, grow them in the same ground as the damaged ones for at least two years.

Verticillium wilt. This disease is apparent in a number of ways, sometimes affecting lower leaves only.

CHRYSANTHEMUM PESTS

Aphids (greenfly and blackfly)

There are ten or more types of aphids that attack chrysanthemums. By sucking the sap they cause serious distortion to foliage and young shoots, although their real danger is that they are carriers of aspermy virus disease. They must, therefore, be dealt with promptly by spraying with B.H.C., nicotine, liquid derris, malathion or diazitol. To prevent the risk of a resistance being set up by the insects, it is best to change from one insecticide to another during the season.

Capsid bugs

There are two species of capsid bug, quite similar to each other in size and general appearance, being green in colour, and slightly larger than a house fly. One is called the Capsid Bug and the other the Tarnished Plant Bug (or Bishop Bug). Although they differ in their habits, the result of their activities is much the same. Their attacks result in blind shoots, distorted stems, mottled foliage and badly shaped flowers. One sided blooms can be an indication of their depredation.

Like adult frog-hoppers, they are difficult to control because they penetrate the shoots and stems. The young unopened distorted buds should be sprayed with wettable DDT, which is probably the best remedy known today. When the insects are disturbed, they do not hop like frog-hoppers, but run along the stalks, finally falling off. If the ground beneath the plants is sprinkled with DDT powder, they will then be killed.

Often, in July and August, capsid bugs appear in the garden in large numbers. It is then a good idea to spray nearby long grass and hedges with Lindex or Sybol. Control in greenhouses can be achieved with low pressure aerosols of malathion.

Chrysanthemum leaf eelworm

Eelworms, a type of nematode, are among the more serious pests and can cause immense damage to plants in a short space of time. There are several species which attack a great variety of plants; however, *Aphelenchoides ritzema-bosi* confines its activi-

Aphids (Greenfly and Blackfly)

Capsid bug damage. *(Right)*
Distorted blooms. *(Below)*
Damaged stalk.

ties to chrysanthemums. This species of eelworm is microscopic and enters plants through the minute breathing pores devouring the green tissues first, forming brown blotches which spread and turn black. The leaves subsequently fall off.

Eelworms are transported up the stems and along the laterals in a film of water. Their attacks, which usually occur in August, are intensified in wet weather.

There is no sure cure for eelworm in the soil, although it is possible to free stools and cuttings from them. Even then, replanting the cuttings in soil containing eelworms soon results in re-infection. Commercially, and especially in the event of a severe attack, this pest is controlled by rotation of crops, growing plants on fresh ground every three years.

Stools, when lifted, can be freed from eelworm by washing off the soil and immersing them for 5 minutes in water at a temperature of $115°F$.

Chrysanthemum leaf miner

The Chrysanthemum Leaf Miner is a small, brown fly, not unlike a house fly. The adult insect is seldom seen, but its maggot, unless steps are taken to destroy the fly, shows its presence quite markedly. Since the fly mounts its attack when the cuttings are being rooted, it is imperative to take action then. The female fly bores into the leaf and lays eggs singly between the upper and lower skins. The egg hatches and

Typical appearance of leaf miner.

132

Appearance of plant attacked by leaf eelworm.

the maggot, if undisturbed, becomes a fly, and in its turn lays an egg. The presence of maggots is shown by white dots on the upper surface of the leaves.

Badly attacked leaves appear to be covered with snaky white lines which, on closer inspection, prove to be the tunnels left by the grubs in their passage through the leaves. If the lower sides of the leaves are looked at, the fully grown maggot, about $\frac{1}{8}$ inch long, can be seen. It can be killed by crushing.

As the maggots are protected by the skin of the leaves they are difficult to destroy with insecticides. The major objective in control, therefore, must be the fly itself, before it lays its eggs. This can be done by fumigating the greenhouse with nicotine or B.H.C. Alternatively, malathion or diazitol may be used as a spray. Care should be taken to see that the nicotine fumigant is not too strong, otherwise it will scorch the margins of the leaves. Maggots in stools and cuttings can be destroyed by spraying with Lindex or Sybol. The concentration of these should not be too high, otherwise scabs or dead patches are likely to develop. Leaves damaged by leaf miner maggots should be destroyed without delay.

Earwigs do enormous damage to opening blooms. DDT is effective, but the best method of protection is to smear 'Vaseline' around the stem below the bud.

Froghoppers do similar damage to capsid bugs and can be controlled with DDT.

Earwigs

These familiar insects do a great deal of damage which is sometimes wrongly attributed to other causes. Earwigs are particularly partial to petals, which they devour greedily, giving blooms a very ragged appearance. They also attack leaves and buds, especially in greenhouses. As earwigs are nocturnal it is not surprising that they often go undetected.

There are two ways to combat this pest. Firstly, by making use of their love of dark hiding places, and secondly, by poisoning them with a suitable bait. Traps can be made by inverting small, hay-stuffed flower pots on canes, by placing old, hollow broad bean stalks in the branches of the plant attacked or by suspending slightly opened match boxes from them. DDT lightly dusted on the leaves is the best preventive.

In addition to the above measures, earwigs can be prevented from entering the blooms by spreading a band of 'Vaseline' around the stem just below the flower head.

Frog-hoppers

These pests attack chrysanthemums at two stages. In June, they appear in the nymph stage in the familiar cuckoo-spit, when they suck the sap from the lower surface of the leaf, hindering the plant's growth and causing the leaves to curl up.

Later, the adult frog-hopper takes over the destruction. It is a brown insect, about $\frac{1}{4}$ inch long with a hard and scaly wing covering. If disturbed it characteristically leaps about. It punctures the young stalks, just below the bud, and sucks the sap. The flower develops at right-angles to the stem, rather similar to the effect produced by capsid bugs. Shorter florets are apparent where the attack has been mounted.

It is imperative to destroy the insects at the nymph stage. Once adults, they bury themselves in buds and become difficult to kill. Lindex or Sybol, used as a spray, is very effective. Wettable DDT spray is of value in controlling the adult frog-hoppers. They are more easily caught in early morning when their wings and surroundings are wet with dew, which retards their vaulting activities.

In recent years, low pressure aerosols containing Malathion, primarily intended for saturating the atmosphere of a greenhouse, have been introduced. They have proved very effective, destroying both frog-hoppers and capsid bugs in flight.

Slugs and snails

These are well known garden pests and are usually present in every garden. Surprisingly enough, slugs seem to be destructive in inverse proportion to their size; the small grey and

Snails and slugs can be controlled by a number of poisons as explained in the text.

black species do far greater damage. Slugs and snails are for the most part night workers, and by day they hide in dark crannies or in the soil. In consequence their depredations are often wrongly blamed upon some other creature. A search after dark with the aid of a torch will usually set doubts at rest. The appearance of ragged holes in the leaves of plants, sometimes with tell-tale slime trails leading to them, will warn the more experienced gardener what he is up against.

Fortunately there are a number of excellent slug poisons on the market. Two first-class recipes which can be made at home are powdered metaldehyde mixed with bran, and Paris Green with bran. To 3 pounds of bran use 1 ounce of metaldehyde finely crushed or 2 ounces of Paris Green. Sprinkle either bait around plants liable to be attacked or place in small heaps where the slugs can get at it. The Paris Green bait has the disadvantage of being poisonous to human beings and domestic animals. Both baits are most effective if used in damp, warm weather. Metaldehyde can also be obtained in suspension. It is then mixed with water and applied to soil and plants from a watering can fitted with a rose.

Thrips

These are slender insects with stout, cone-shaped mouth-parts. They rasp or scrape the stem or leaf of a plant, then suck out the sap that flows into the wound. Most species have narrow, bristle-like fringed wings. They cause damage to chrysanthemums, both as almost transparent minute nymphs and as adults when they are tiny and black. As minute nymphs they appear on the undersides of the leaves in hot, dry and thundery weather, producing mottled leaves and stunted growth. The fully grown thrips frequent the florets of half and fully opened blooms. This results in the shrivelling and drooping of their outer florets, especially when there has been a spell of hot weather.

Thrips, at both stages in their life cycle, are destroyed by DDT, Lindex and Sybol sprays. It is important to treat the lower surface of the leaves, as it is there that the insects congregate. Apart from the damage they cause to the plant, they are carriers of spotted wilt disease, and they must therefore be destroyed.

An aerosol spray can be used to create a protective atmosphere in the greenhouse It is inadvisable to allow the spray to fall directly on to the foliage because of the risk of leaf scorch caused by the propellant liquid.

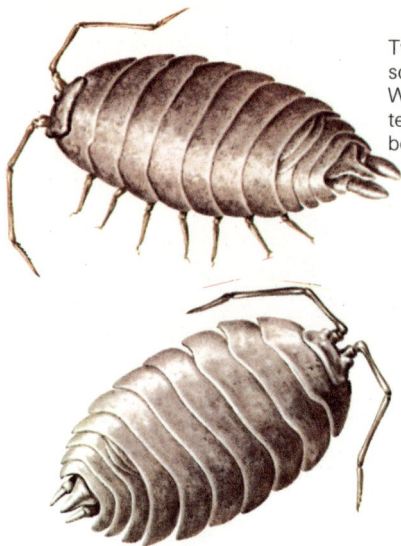

Two species of woodlouse, sometimes called 'pillbugs'. When disturbed they characteristically coil up as shown below.

Wireworms

These are to be found everywhere, and are amongst the most destructive soil pests in the garden. They are the larvae of certain species of small brown beetles, known as 'click beetles'. The wireworms themselves are yellow, shiny-skinned, up to an inch long and no thicker than a piece of ordinary string. They are not very active and have only three pairs of small legs near the head. Wireworms live on the roots of plants and are particularly fond of potatoes and carrots, a fact which is useful to know when planning an attack on them. They devour chrysanthemum roots and may also attack the stems. Sometimes they bore right inside the stem of a young plant. The first sign of this will be the leaves drooping. Eventually the plant will die.

Good cultivation will reduce the wireworm population by exposing the grubs to birds. Alternatively, they can be trapped in a sliced potato or carrot buried just beneath the surface of the soil near a plant and examined every day or so for visitors. Potting and seed soil may be sterilised by heat or with one of the advertised chemical sterilisers.

An insecticide containing lindane may also be applied to the soil according to the manufacturer's instructions.

Woodlice

Every gardener will be familiar with this little grey or black creature that has the habit of rolling itself into a ball when disturbed. For this reason it is sometimes called a 'pillbug'. It feeds mainly on decaying matter but will attack young shoots growing from stools in frames or greenhouses, which may be eaten off so cleanly that they have the appearance of being mown. Many can be trapped in the same way as earwigs (see page 134) and they can also be poisoned with a mixture of Paris Green and bran as advised for slugs and snails (see page 135), or 1 ounce of Paris Green mixed with 3 pounds of dried blood. Another effective remedy is 5 per cent DDT or B.H.C. dust sprinkled where they are seen. In greenhouses fumigation with B.H.C. or DDT is effective. Decaying refuse should be removed as it provides a hiding place and breeding ground.

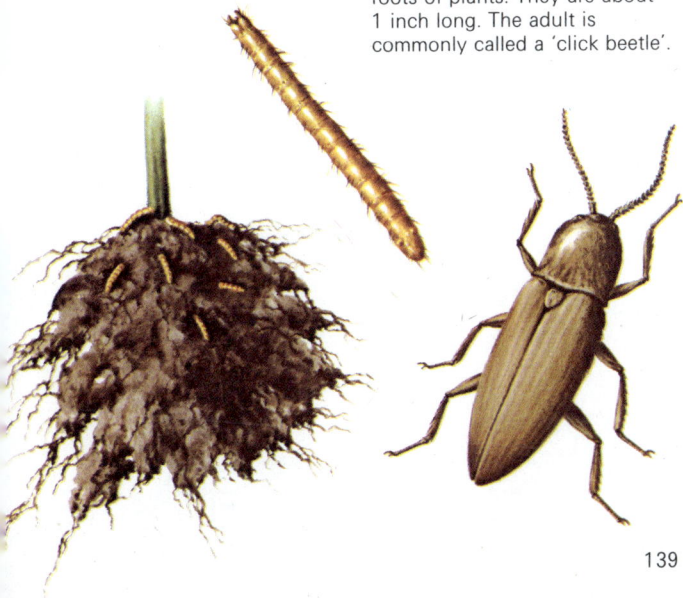

Wireworms, as shown, attack the roots of plants. They are about 1 inch long. The adult is commonly called a 'click beetle'.

EXHIBITING CHRYSANTHEMUMS

Enthusiastic growers of chrysanthemums often become keen exhibitors. Usually, their first introduction to showing is at a local show. Sometimes this keen interest is confined to early-flowering chrysanthemums, but more often, after gaining experience, the beauty and value of the late-flowering varieties for decorative purposes during the winter impels them to invest in a small greenhouse.

To be a successful exhibitor of chrysanthemums is within the ability of all gardeners. The key to success is to be able to judge and assess the qualities required of a perfect bloom. Prospective exhibitors are advised to consult the publications of the National Chrysanthemum Society. These set down for every class the standard of quality expected and the common faults seen at shows. It is, of course, impossible to give full particulars here, but the following is an extract from *The Chrysanthemum Manual* (Second Revised Edition, 1964), on late-flowering exhibition incurved chrysanthemums.

'Standard of Quality: An incurved bloom should be as nearly a globe as possible. The florets should be broad, smooth, rounded at the tip and of sufficient length to form a graceful curve; they ought to be regularly arranged, firm and close, fresh and the colour clear and decisive. A tightly incurved bloom, which has depth, is superior to a large flattish flower, which has looseness.

Common Faults: Florets loosely incurved, staleness of outer florets; hollow centre; roughness of florets and unevenness of outline; breadth without corresponding depth.'

It may be of value to the would-be exhibitor to know how a judge assesses the merits of this type of early- and late-flowering chrysanthemum.

Form	30
Size	25
Freshness and firmness of florets	25
Colour	10
Foliage	5
Staging	5
Total	100

A vase of five early-flowering reflexed decoratives arranged for the show bench. Blooms are broad, deep and full in the centre. Colour is bright and fresh to the tips of the florets. Points are also given for the quality of foliage—spraying with 'Combinex' gives excellent results. The cultivars here are two Early Red Cloak, two Eva Gray and one Value. NCSC 24b

ENTRY
VASE OF FIVE
DECORATIVES

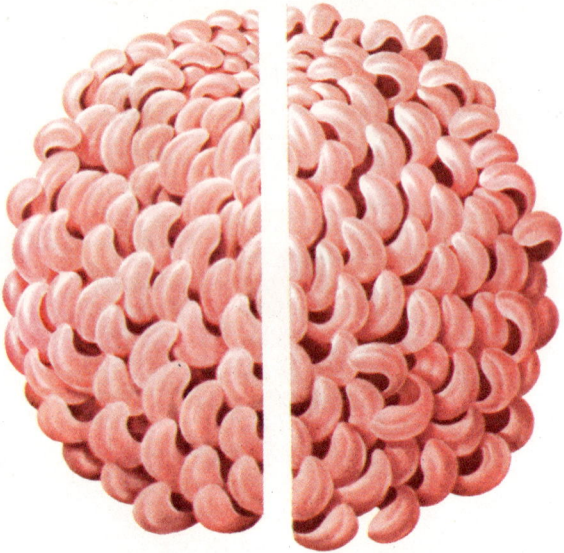

A bloom ready for the show should retain its original character, overdressing being avoided. Untidy florets can, with care, be coaxed into place. The bloom illustrated above has the left side dressed by gently rolling a knitting needle under misplaced florets. Practise on a sub-standard bloom.

It is particularly important to note the high rating given to freshness in this schedule.

With such information the enthusiast is equipped with a knowledge of what is required for successful exhibiting.

Probably the most important thing, apart from the proper cultivation of his plants, that the chrysanthemum exhibitor has to learn, is to be a first-class showman – to display his wares to the best advantage.

It is, of course, necessary to decide a few weeks before the show what classes it is likely to be possible to enter. This entails reading the schedule and assessing which blooms are likely to be at the peak of their perfection on the morning of the show.

For chrysanthemums to be at their best on the show bench

their tissues must be well-filled with water. To be sure of this, it is necessary to stand them up to their necks in cold water for at least twelve hours. They are best cut in the early morning, after being well-watered on the previous evening. Cut the blooms the morning of the day prior to the show. As soon as the flowers are picked, all the lower leaves must be removed, as those beneath the water will deprive the blooms of their water supply and cause bacterial decomposition. It is advisable to crush, scrape or split the ends of the stalks, particularly as some cultivars do not absorb water readily.

Having picked the best blooms, they should be carefully examined to see how near they approach the standard required for successful exhibiting. As mentioned previously, considerable help in this respect can be obtained from the publications of the National Chrysanthemum Society. There is one unfailing rule that must be remembered – the blooms must always be sparkling fresh. Even if slightly smaller, an absolutely fresh flower will always gain points over an enormous one which is fading. Sometimes, if the show is on a warm day, it is better to enter a bloom just below its peak of development because it might be in perfect condition when viewed by the judge.

It should be remembered that the judging of a bloom is always done against the highest possible standard for the variety. Thus, when selecting blooms for a class which calls

A plant can absorb water more readily if the stem is crushed as illustrated. Note that the bloom rests on the forearm.

for more than one variety, it is better to pick out smaller ones which are up to standard rather than very much larger flowers of other cultivars, which are not up to the standard for the variety.

In making the selection of blooms, particular attention should be paid to colour. It is well known that variation can occur within a variety. It is very important, therefore, to ensure that the flowers chosen represent truly the colour for that cultivar.

Unlike some flowers, a considerable amount can be done to clean up exhibition chrysanthemums. The blooms should be very carefully examined for blemishes caused by bad weather. Damaged florets should be picked off with a pair of forceps. Old, stale florets which hang down lifeless and close to the stem should be removed. In the case of white chrysanthemums, it is essential to go over them for a second time just before the show, as they tend to develop spotted florets after they have been picked. With late-flowering singles intended for

After stripping off the lower leaves the plant is placed in water. In this case a glass is illustrated to show the water level, but in practice a metal container is used.

Shirley Giant
Late-flowering
large exhibition
NCS Classification 1

(Top) A typical packing arrangement of early chrysanthemums.
Rolls of paper are wedged in to support the necks of the blooms.
The 'tie stick' is shown unwrapped for clarity. *(Bottom)* One dozen
blooms with wrapped tie stick wedged in position. Foliage is not
shown here so that packing can be seen.

November shows, odd ray florets appearing in the centre disc should be pulled out while the blooms are still on the plants, so that there is no gap remaining by the time they are staged.

It should also be remembered that in quite a number of sections foliage counts for points. In such cases, diseased leaves and any damaged by eelworms should be removed.

To show large and medium exhibition cultivars to their best advantage it is permissible to use cups or wires to support them, but they must on no account exceed 3 inches in diameter, including any padding used. No cups or rings are allowed for exhibition incurved varieties, but supports for their stems will not disqualify them. The wire frames used for exhibition cultivars are made of fairly heavy gauge wire, about 20 inches long with a cup or ring formed at the top at right angles to the long axis. Failing to do these things will result in the judge penalising the exhibit.

To fix these wire supports in place, all the foliage must be stripped from the stems. The bloom is held upside down and the wire support tied firmly to the stalk so that when the flower is turned up the right way the florets are resting on the wire ring. This increases the apparent diameter of the bloom by up to as much as 2 inches. This must, however, be done with discretion, because it must be borne in mind that, by definition, exhibition varieties 'should have breadth and depth in equal proportions'. The wire support is finally adjusted correctly in the show-tent. At the same time, additional foliage is tied to the bare flower stem for purely decorative purposes, just before staging.

Early-flowering varieties, decoratives and singles can be packed horizontally in a standard florist's box, which has the dimensions 36 inches long, 18 inches wide and 6 inches deep. The boxes are lined with tissue paper in such a way that there is sufficient overlap at the sides and ends to cover the blooms and prevent them being damaged by rubbing the sides and lid. The necks of the blooms are supported by a roll of corrugated paper or newspaper, about $18\frac{1}{2}$ inches long, so that it fits tightly across the width of the box and about 2 inches in diameter. To support a full box of blooms, four or six rolls are required. To hold the flowers in place during transit, a 'tie stick', made from a bamboo cane a little longer than the width of the box, so that it fits across it tightly, is also needed.

For the purpose of safely transporting large exhibition and exhibition incurved blooms, a special packing case is necessary. This is designed to hold the stems in an upright position by tying them securely to horizontal rails in the case. Such boxes are called 'hurdle boxes'.

It is essential to ensure that the names of the blooms are clearly shown on cards. Also make sure that all the articles you are likely to require at the show are taken with you. These include name cards, the show schedule, a pencil, a pocket knife, secateurs, green string, a large camel-hair brush, short thin canes for lengthening the blooms under water, wire supports, spare foliage (at the November shows), moss for packing in the vases so that the chrysanthemums can be well arranged, a watering can, a bucket and, above all, spare blooms.

For the purpose of illustration this hurdle box has one side removed. The blooms are normally packed when the hurdle is in position. The stems are wrapped in damp moss to keep the bloom fresh.

As soon as the flowers are unpacked, place them up to their necks in water. Work out how you are going to arrange your blooms before you leave home. Well pack your vases with moss or other suitable material so that the stems are kept in position. In a five bloom class it is advisable to have three fairly high up with two on shorter stems towards the front. As far as possible, ensure that the colours do not clash in exhibits which call for more than one cultivar. When you are absolutely satisfied, put them in the place allotted to you on the show-bench.

Finally, collect your show cards and place them downwards in the front of your entry, together with the name cards. Before you take this final step, be absolutely sure that your exhibit is as you want it, because once you have placed your exhibitor's card on the bench you are not allowed to move your blooms to adjust them without the permission of the show secretary.

Exhibition blooms are permitted to have wire ring supports. The ring is placed in position with the plant upside down. Foliage can also be added for decoration.

The interior of this large commercial greenhouse is fully equipped for all-year-round chrysanthemums. It has overhead irrigation, mercury vapour lighting and blinds.

CHRYSANTHEMUMS ALL THE YEAR ROUND

A practice mainly applicable to commercial growers and probably the most important development in the growing techniques of chrysanthemums in recent years is the production of blooms at all times of the year.

This is based on the discovery made nearly fifty years ago that the development of flower buds on various types of plants is related to the length of the daylight hours. Mid-season and late-flowering chrysanthemums, but not earlies, will produce buds only when the day is less than $14\frac{1}{2}$ hours long, and the buds will develop into flowers when there are less than $13\frac{1}{2}$ hours of daylight. They are, therefore, defined as 'short day' plants. When blooming naturally, mid-season and late-flowering chrysanthemums develop from buds formed from mid-August onwards and flower at varying times throughout the winter during which period the length of the days conforms to those mentioned above.

These facts can be used to control the flowering dates of chrysanthemums. Thus, by artificially extending the length of the day by exposing the plants to electric lighting, vegetative growth will continue, but budding will be retarded. In practice, commercial growers prefer to shorten the night by switching on the lights for a period during the hours of darkness, rather than continuing the exposure at the end of the day. On the other hand, if buds and flowers are wanted during the long summer days, the period of daylight is shortened by screening the plants with curtains, made of black cloth or polythene.

If other conditions, like temperature, water supply, feeding, soil texture and so on are also regularly controlled, flowers can be obtained with suitably long stems at any time throughout the year. To do this, growers equip their glasshouses with banks of 100-watt incandescent lamps, placed 4 feet 6 inches above the beds. These are switched on automatically for varying periods, controlled by a time switch. The beds of plants also have continuous black curtains, which are used to shorten the day length when necessary, and to prevent light penetrating into areas where it is not wanted.

MONTHLY PROGRAMME

The beginner may find the following programme useful in that it summarizes the more important tasks to be undertaken month by month.

January

Weather permitting, the ground should be dug and humus, such as well-rotted farmyard manure or garden compost, added. Cold frames should be checked to ensure adequate weather protection of stools; also see that there have been no slug attacks. Indoors, continue to take cuttings of indoor varieties. Rooting can be aided with the use of hormone powder. Labels should be dated as this may be important later.

Now is the time to order both indoor and outdoor varieties from the nurseries. When the cuttings arrive they should be potted. If they cannot be handled at once they should be unpacked and stood upright in water. If they are plants dip the foliage only *not* the roots and then proceed as for cuttings. Again, label as you go along.

February

Cuttings should be fed with liquid manure or some other food. Healthy stools of both early and late varieties can be brought into the slight warmth of the greenhouse. Pot on into 3-inch pots cuttings of large exhibition varieties that were taken in December and January. Compost can now be prepared for potting during the coming weeks. Some pests also come to life in this month so keep a watch for slugs and leaf miners.

March

Pot on into 3-inch pots cuttings of all varieties that were taken in January or February. Canes should be inserted into the pots so that top-heavy plants do not bend. The stopping table will need to be consulted regularly from now on. If the weather is good, hardening-off can commence by increasing greenhouse ventilation. Later, the first batch can be put into cold frames, but beware of frosts and always cover well at night. Plants will need more watering as they grow, but only sparingly. When frame watering is necessary do it before midday. Cuttings can still be taken from earlies, as they root, box them without overcrowding.

April
This is a busy month with plants requiring a lot of attention. Over watering must be avoided, but regular watering is important as well as plenty of light and air. As the plants grow give them as much room as possible. Hardening-off continues but beware of late frosts. Sites can now be prepared for earlies.

May
Depending upon the weather, earlies should be ready for planting out during the last two weeks of this month. Lates should be transplanted into their final pots about the end of the second week in readiness for putting out into the open at the beginning of June. Strictly speaking, stopping commences during this month. The stopping tables should be consulted.

If stopping does commence, it is well to remember that only well rooted plants should be stopped. If the roots are disturbed when repotting into final pots the plant should be given time to recover before the stopping takes place.

June
For general garden purposes, stop earlies, that normally bloom on the first-crown bud, by pinching out the tips of the main stems early this month. Spray varieties and others that bloom from second-crown buds will require to be stopped again at the end of the month. Exceptions to this procedure are the Christmas flowering varieties, which should be pinched early in the month and again in middle or late July. Normal garden maintenance should continue in earnest.

July
Earlies will require disbudding. Late-flowering varieties in pots will require feeding and the use of a balanced fertilizer is recommended.

Sap-sucking pests rear their heads about now. They are particularly partial to buds, so constant attention is required. Christmas varieties will require their second stop as directed in the tables.

August

Earlies may need further disbudding and some will begin to show colour. Earwigs may be a problem this month.

Lates will still require feeding and will begin to show buds. Large exhibition varieties should be secured about the middle of the month. Full details are given in the section on stopping.

September

Earlies should now be in full colour and notes should be made of the plants, which must be perfectly healthy, required for propagation. Now is a good time to prepare the greenhouse for lates. Plants should be 'tidied up' by removing lower leaves and shoots and sprayed with insecticide about the middle of the month. Housing should commence about the 20th, particularly if colour is showing in the bud.

Plants should have their last feed and canes cut to the requisite length, if necessary. Every plant should be sprayed with a fungicide and inspected for disease or damage before it is brought into the house; diseased plants should be burned. The tallest plants should be housed first and care should be taken to avoid crowding. When complete the house should be fumigated and thereafter about once a week.

October

If the weather is good continue to ventilate freely but towards the middle of the month it may be necessary to close down a little at night and provide some heating to keep the air dry. Large fluctuation between day and night temperatures should be avoided if possible, the temperature being kept at about 13°C (55°F). Ventilators should not be completely closed as it is important to keep the air circulating.

November

Lates should now be in bloom and chosen plants should be marked for propagation. Christmas blooms should be kept fairly cool until flowers show. Frames can be prepared for stools of earlies which should be lifted about now. Roots should be kept moist, but do not over water. Take cuttings of plants required to produce large specimen plants. Canes should be collected, thoroughly washed and stored in a dry place.

If eelworm is troublesome, stools should be immersed in a warm water bath at 115°F for five minutes. This should be done early as it will take time if the trouble is widespread.

December

Christmas plants will be in bloom and should be given some ventilation on mild days. Take cuttings of large exhibition varieties during this month and January. Those to be grown on second crown buds must be taken early this month. Before doing so the stools should be sprayed with insecticide.

BOOKS TO READ

For general books on the subject, the following are recommended and are usually available from bookshops or public libraries.

Chrysanthemums edited by A. G. L. Hellyer. Collingridge, London, 1963.

Chrysanthemums by H. G. W. Fogg. Parrish, London, 1966.

Chrysanthemums for Everyone by F. W. Loads. Foyle, 1963.

Chrysanthemums for Gardens and Home Decoration by A. G. Carpenter. The National Chrysanthemum Society, 1964.

Chrysanthemums for Garden and Exhibition by J. Woolman. Collingridge, London, 1964.

Chrysanthemums for Small Gardens by J. F. Smith. Pan Books, London, 1966.

Chrysanthemum Growing by H. G. W. Fogg. Gifford, London, 1962.

Chrysanthemum Growers' Treasury by J. H. Goddard. Revised by E. Morley Jones. Collingridge, London, 1963.

The Chrysanthemum Manual. The National Chrysanthemum Society, 1969.

Chrysanthemum Stopping and Timing. The National Chrysanthemum Society, 1968.

Cultivation of Outdoor Chrysanthemums for Amateurs. The National Chrysanthemum Society.

Dahlias and Chrysanthemums by Percy Thrower. Collingridge, London, 1967.

Early Flowering Chrysanthemums by E. Morley Jones. Collingridge, London, 1967.

Garden Chrysanthemums by Carpenter and Snelling. Collingridge, London, 1964.

Pests and Diseases of the Chrysanthemum by E. Morley Jones. The National Chrysanthemum Society, London, 1966.

Soilless Composts for Chrysanthemums by E. Morley Jones. The National Chrysanthemum Society, London, 1966.

Starting with Chrysanthemums by E. Morley Jones. Collingridge, London, 1966.

INDEX

Page numbers in bold type
refer to illustrations. The
names of varieties are listed
alphabetically under
'varieties'.

Aerosols 130, 135, **137**
Ammonium nitrate 30
Ammonium sulphate 30
Anemones **16**, 18, 117
Aphids 122, 130, **131**
Aspermy 122, **126**, 130

B.H.C. (Lindane) 130, 133,
139
Bishop Bug 130
Blackfly 130, **131**
Bonemeal 30, 59
Bordeaux mixture 127
Boron 26, 29
Botrytis 122
Break bud 55

Calcium 26, 27, 60
Capsid bugs 130, 134
Captan 122
Carbon cycle, the **37**
Cascades **19**, 20, 121
Charm chrysanthemums **17**,
20, 23, 94, **94**, **95**, 120,
120
Chlorosis **28**, 29
Chrysanthemum Manual,
The 140, 156
Chrysanthemum maximum
11, 21, 97
Chrysanthemum rubellum
11, **11**, 21, 22, 92
Chusan Daisy 9
Click beetle 139
Composts, potting 35–41
Copper 26
Corynebacterium fasciens
123
Counting down 58
Crown and leafy gall 123
Cuckoo-spit 135
Cuttings
    Planting distances 47, 48,
    48
    Root (basal) 44, 46, **46**
    Rooting a small number
    52, 53
    Rooting compounds 47,
    47, 152
    Stem 46, **46**

Taking and rooting
45–53, **45**, 49
Time of rooting 43

Damping 27, 107
DDT 130, 134, 135, 136,
139
Decoratives 16, 17, 22, 43
Derris 100, 130
Diazitol 130, 133
Disbudding 58, 70
Diseases 122–129
    Aspermy 122, **126**, 130
    Botrytis 122
    Crown and leafy gall 123
    Mildew 124, **124**
    Rust 122–123, **123**
    Septoria leaf spot 125,
    128
    Spotted wilt **126**, 127,
    136
    Verticillium wilt 128, **129**
    Virus 122
Dried blood 30, 139
Dwarf pot plants 119–120

Early-flowering chrysan-
themums 12, 17, 23, **40**,
45, 86–97
Earwigs 134, **134**, 154
Eelworm 130, **133**, 155
Erysiphe cichoracearum 124
Exhibiting 140–149
    Arranging the blooms 149
    Cutting blooms 143
    Dressing a bloom **142**,
    144
    Equipment needed at
    show 148
    Hurdle boxes 148, **148**
    Packing blooms for
    transporting **146**, 147,
    148, **148**
    Preparing blooms for
    showing **142**, 143,
    143, **144**, 144, 147
    Selecting blooms 142,
    143, 144
    Standards of quality 140
    Judging 140
    Wire supports 147, **149**
Exhibition chrysanthemums
12
Exhibition incurved 12, 16,
43, 109–110

Farmyard manure 29, 33,
34, 59, 70, 152
Feeding 24–29
Fertilizers 29–34
First crown buds 55, **57**, 71,
73, 75, 76, 81, 112, 113,
114
Frog-hoppers 130, **134**, 135

Garden compost 33, 35, 152
Garden display, chrysan-
themums for 86
Greenfly 130, **131**

Heat therapy 24
Hoof and horn meal 30, 38,
41
Hops, spent 33, 70
Housing **102**, 106, 154
Hurdle boxes 148, **148**

Incurved decoratives 17, 78
Incurving chrysanthemums
12, 16
Intermediate decoratives 17,
112
Iron 26, 29

John Innes Base Fertilizer
38, 59
John Innes Potting Com-
posts 35, 36–40, 41, 99
John Innes 'L' Feed 69

Karathane 125
Korean chrysanthemums 5,
11, **17**, 20, 22, 90, 91

Large exhibition chrysan-
themums 12, 43,
103–107
Late-flowering chrysan-
themums 12, 17, 23,
98–121
Leaf miner 132, **132**, 152
Leaves, yellowing **28**, 29
Lime 29, 41, **61**
Lime, carbonate of 29, 60, **61**
Lindane (B.H.C.) 100, 138
Lindex 130, 133, 135, 136
Loam **34**, **35**, 38

Magnesium 26, **28**, 29
Malathion 100, 130, 133,
135

Manganese 26, **28**, 29
Meat and bonemeal 30
Medium exhibitions 12, 108
Metaldehyde 136
Mildew 124, **124**

National Chrysanthemum
  Society 6, 43, 70, 103,
  140, 156
Natural break 55, 72, 73,
  76, 79, 81, 103, 104, 108
Natural break bud 55
Nicotine 130, 133
Nitrogen 25, 26, 27, 30, **32**,
  33, 69, 122
Nitrogen cycle, the **32**

Paraquat 68
Paris Green 136, 139
Peat 36, 38, 39, 40, 59, **61**
Pests 130–139
Phosphate 26, 30, 33, 69
Phosphorus 26, 27
Photosynthesis 24, **31**, 37
pH Value 29, 35, 59, 60, **61**
Pillbugs **138**, 139
Plant nutrients, sources of
  30, 33
Pompons 9, **16**, 18, 22, 43,
  86–88, **86**, **87**, 117
Potash 26, 33, 38
Potassium 26, 27, **28**, 69
Potassium nitrate 33, 41
Potassium sulphate 33, 38
Potting procedure **98**,
  99–101, **99**
Poultry manure 33, 59
Propagation 43–53, 154.
Puccinia chrysanthemi 122

Rayonnantes 5, **14**, 20
Reflexed decoratives 17, 112
Reflexing chrysanthemums
  12, 16
Running on 55, 98
Rubellums 11, **11**, 21, 22, 92
Rust 122–123, **123**

Sand 36, 38, 39, 40
Second-crown buds 55, **58**,
  98, 112, 113, 114
Securing **57**, 58, 71, 75, **75**
Septoria chrysanthemella
  125
Septoria leaf spot 125, **128**
Septoria obesa 125
Sequestrene-plus **28**, 29
Sewage sludge 33, 59

Simazine 68
Singles 19, 43, 114
Slugs 135, **135**, 152
Snails 135, **135**
Sodium nitrate 30
Soil, alkaline 29, 59
Soilless composts 40
Soil testing 26, 29, 60, **61**
Soot 30
Species
  Chrysanthemum alpinum
    10, **10**
  C. argenteum **9**, 10
  C. articum 10
  C. azaleanum 5, 10
  C. catanache 10
  C. coccineum 8
  C. erubescens 10
  C. frutescens 8
  C. indicum 8, **8**
  C. koreanum 11, **17**, 20,
    22, 90
  C. leucanthemum 11
  C. macrophyllum 11
  C. morifolium 8
  C. mauvii 11
  C. maximum 11, **11**, 21,
    97
  C. rubellum 11, **11**, 21,
    22, 92
  C. sinense 8, **8**
  C. uliginosum 4, 10
Specimen plants 118, **118**,
  119
Spoon chrysanthemums 21,
  90
Spotted wilt **126**, 127, 136
Spray chrysanthemums
  88–89, **88**, **89**
Starch 25, **31**
Stools, aftercare of 41–42,
  42, 152, 155
Sulphur 26, 123
Superphosphate 30, 38, 41
Sybol 130, 133, 135, 136

Tarnished plant bug 130
Thiram 123
Threadworms 130
Thrips 136
Timing 56, 58, 71, **73**
Trace elements 26, 29

Varieties
  Ada Miles 91
  Albert Shoesmith 104
  Alec Bedser 81
  Amber Long Island
    Beauty 117
  Anna Hay 92
  Ann, Lady Brockett 92

Apricot Charming 89
Arthur Blythe 104, **107**
Ashover Atom 78
Atco 117
Audrey Shoesmith 110
Autumn Shirley 115
Beeswing 87
Ben Lomond 97
Bessie Rowe **74**
Betty 91
Betty Rose 117
Birmingham 108
Blazing Gold 110
Blondie 91
Bob 87
Brenda Talbot **78**, 81
Broadway **26**
Bronze Covent Garden **84**
Bronze Fairie 87
Bronze Gremlin 87
Buff Maylen 110
Cameo 87
Camp Fire 81
Capstan 79
Charming **89**
Charm Spoon 90
Cheerful **115**
Chesswood Beauty 115
Clara Curtis **93**
Claretglow 81
Cobham Gold **96**, 97
Connie Mayhew 108
Coquette 91
Cossack 108, **109**
Cricket 81
Crimson Betty Rose **116**,
  117
Darkie 81
Deep Crimson **121**
Delightful 81
Denebola 117
Denise 87, **87**
Desert Song **114**, 115
Dexta 110
Donna 110
Doone Valley 81
Dresden China 117
Droitwich Beauty 97
Duchess of Edinburgh 92
Duke of Kent 104, **105**
Early Red Cloak **141**
Elspeth 117
Ermine 78
Esther Read 11, 97
Ethel Edmonds 81
Eva Gray **141**
Evelyn Bush 81
Everest 97
Eye Catcher 79
Fair Dinkum 81
Fair Lady **113**
Fortyniner 117

Francis Jefferson 110, **111**
Garden White 89
Garnet Spoon 90
Gay Cavalier 77
Gert Raynor 91
Gigantic 104
Gipsy **13**, 79
Glenshades **112**
Glen Fire 81
Glint 91
Golden Boy 81
Golden Curry **119**
Golden Orfe **88**, 89
Golden Seal 115
Gold Lust 91
Gretal 90
Goude Elsje 89
Grace Land 117
Graham Knight **63**
Greatness 79
Gremlin 87
Harold Habgood 104
Helga Taylor **77**
Henley 78
Herbert Cuerdon 110
Herb Miles 91
Honeyglow 79
Imp 86, **87**
Ivy Joice 91
James Bryant **14**, 104
Jante Wells 87
Jessie Cooper 92
Jessie Habgood 104
Jim Plummer 79
Jim Stacey 108
Joan Reeves 97
Joe Edwards **63**
John Murray 97
John Rowe 110
John Shoesmith 79
John Woolman **13**, 81
Joke 89
J. S. Dakers 104
Kansas 79
Kathleen Doward 81
Keith Riley 78
Keystone **25**, 81
Leslie Thomas **62**, 81
Lilac Prince 104
Lilian Hoek 89
Lilian Jackson **18**
Lilian Smallwood 104
Lilian Shoesmith 110
Long Island Beauty 117
Lustre 87
Magna Carta 110
Maria Shoesmith **111**
Mark Woolman 104
Martin Riley **74**, 78
Mary Rowe 110
Mary Stoker 92

Masquerade 87
Mavis Shoesmith 110
Maylen **15**, 110
Mdlle Elise Dordan 117
Melody 91
Minstrel Boy 110
Monica Bennett 104
Monica Winterton 108
Moonlight 97
Moonlight Spoon 90
Morley Jones 81
Nancy Matthews 78
Nancy Sherwood 115
Nautilus 115
Nebula 117
Niagara **19**
Noon 91
November Bronze 117
November Midget 117
Orange 89
Orchid Beauty 117
Otley Beauty **90**, 91
Patricia Bennett 104
Paul Boissier 92
Paul Habgood **105**
Peggy Stevens 115
Peter May 104, **106**
Peter Shoesmith 79
Phyllis Smith 97
Pink Cloud 110
Pink Glory 89
Pink Thomas Bestwick **77**
Picolino 87
Popcorn 117
Preference 115
Primrose Long Island
  Beauty 117
Prince Charles 92
Princess Anne **21**
Princess Margaret 92
Raymond Mounsey 117
Red Ensign 92
Red Rolinda 117
Red Setter 81, **84**
Red Pye 89
Regalia 81
Rip Joice 91
Rita Shirley **108**, 108
Rita Tench 91
Rolinda 117
Ron Shoesmith 110, **110**
Rosamund Noble 79
Rosette Queen 89
Saint Edmundsbury 104
Shining Light 90
Shirley Crystal 110
Shirley Giant **145**
Shirley Model 110
Shirley Sunshine 115
Silver Dollar **27**
Silver Knight 110
Snowball 97

Sonnegold 89
Souvenir 110
Stan Joice 91
Starfire 81
Startler 91
Sulphur Long Island
  Beauty 117
Sunrise 91
Super Star 79
Susan Maughan 81
Sussex Yellow **127**
Thomas Killan **15**, 97
Tickled Pink 90
Tipoff 89
Tombola **13**
Topper 78, **79**
Troef 89
Tracy Waller **62**, 79
Twinkle 91
Vagabond 92
Value **141**
Vera Woolman 110
Wally Ruff 89
Walter Warner 110
Waterloo 110
Welcome News 110
Westfield Bronze 81
White Spoon 90
Winn Quinn 108
Wirral Pride 97
Wirral Supreme 11, 97
Woking Rose 104
Woolman's Glory 115
Woolman's Perfecta 110
Woolman's Victor 104
Wychwood 115
Yellow Bickleigh 110
Yellow Brocade 110
Yellow Hammer 120
Yellow Long Island
  Beauty 117
Yellow Marvel 110
Yellow Nuggett 78
Yellow Rolinda 117
Yellow Ron Shoesmith
  110
Yellow Tench 91
Vernalization 42
Verticillium wilt 128, **129**
Virus diseases 122, 127

Watering **71**, **101**
Weldmesh **67**
Wire mesh supports 66
Wireworms 138, **139**
Wood ash 33
Woodlice **138**, 139

Zinc 26

MONTHS AND SEASONS

The months and seasons mentioned in this book apply to temperate regions of the northern hemisphere (Europe, Canada and the northern United States). For readers living in other regions, the following table gives approximate equivalents.

Subtropical regions of the northern hemisphere (Mediterranean sea, southern United States)

Plants will tend to shoot and flower a month or so earlier in these regions.

Tropical regions (around the equator)

No seasons exist in the tropical regions. There are no set times for planting, and the suitability of growing an individual plant will depend on local climatic conditions.

Subtropical regions of the southern hemisphere (Australasia, South America, southern Africa)

The seasons are reversed in these regions. Spring is approximately from September to November, summer from December to February, autumn from March to May, and winter from June to August.

SOME OTHER TITLES IN THIS SERIES

Natural History

Bird Behaviour
Fishes of the World
Fossil Man
Life in the Sea
Natural History Collecting
The Plant Kingdom
Prehistoric Animals
Seashores
Snakes of the World
Wild Cats

Gardening

Flower Arranging
Garden Flowers
Garden Shrubs

General Information

Sailing Ships
Sea Fishing
Trains

Popular Science

Atomic Energy
Computers at Work
Electronics
Mathematics
The Weather Guide

Arts

Architecture
Jewellery
Porcelain

Domestic Animals and Pets

Budgerigars
Pets for Children